HOT PRAISE FOR

Curves Rule and
Flat Is Fabulous

"The best fashion and beauty tips."
       —Steven "Cojo" Cojocaru

"Fabulous and inspiring."
       —Susan Kaufman, editor, *People StyleWatch*

"Fun and empowering. Read it and get set to get gorgeously dressed."
       —Bonnie Fuller, author of *The Joys of Much Too Much*

"Ladies, forget about those harsh rules dictating what you can't wear—Elycia and Rita share all of the stylish and flattering clothes you *can* wear!"
       —Tracey Gold, actress

"This book shows you how to love your figure and look fabulous doing it."
       —Marissa Jaret Winokur, actress

Curves Rule

and

Flat Is Fabulous

SEXY, STYLISH LOOKS
FOR EVERY FIGURE

RITA MAUCERI and ELYCIA RUBIN

Photography by Edward Duarte
Illustrations by Naoko Matsunaga

Foreword by MARISSA JARET WINOKUR

CITADEL PRESS
Kensington Publishing Corp.
www.kensingtonbooks.com

CITADEL PRESS BOOKS are published by

Kensington Publishing Corp.
850 Third Avenue
New York, NY 10022

All Kensington titles, imprints, and distributed lines are available at special quantity discounts for bulk purchases for sales promotions, premiums, fund-raising, educational, or institutional use. Special book excerpts or customized printings can also be created to fit specific needs. For details, write or phone the office of the Kensington special sales manager: Kensington Publishing Corp., 850 Third Avenue, New York, NY 10022, attn: Special Sales Department; phone 1-800-221-2647.

CITADEL PRESS and the Citadel logo are Reg. U.S. Pat. & TM Off.

First printing: January 2009

10 9 8 7 6 5 4 3 2 1

Printed in the United States of America

Book design by Anne Ricigliano.

Library of Congress Control Number: 2008936687

ISBN-13: 978-0-8065-2881-6
ISBN-10: 0-8065-2881-8

*W*ithin the last two years, we both had baby girls. There's something about admiring your daughter in all her innocent, chubby glory that makes you realize we aren't born with hang-ups about our bodies—we end up absorbing them as we grow.

When we set out to write this book, we wanted to do something that got women excited and empowered about their figures. We wanted to inspire women to flaunt and flatter what they've got. Since giving birth to our girls, we've gained a little extra padding here and there. Still, we wear it proudly, just like our little girls.

We look at our daughters and marvel at their undeniable sassiness. They stroll around naked like mini goddesses, sticking out their Buddha bellies, swaying their thunder thighs, and shaking their buxom booties. What we wish for them is to always feel that fabulous in their bodies—rolls, dimples, pudge 'n all.

Dedicated to Amalia Grace and Kalya Ever—who are perfect in every way.

—Rita and Elycia

CONTENTS

FOREWORD

by MARISSA JARET WINOKUR

Curves Rule and Flat Is Fabulous goes right along with my "shake what your mama gave you" attitude toward life. I love fashion but I never follow the "rules" dictated by magazines when it comes to picking out what to wear. When stylists have brought me clothes that are three sizes too big to cover my body, I smile politely and tell them "bring me the same clothes you bring the skinny girls—just get them in a larger size."

This book embraces different body types and proves there is no one right way to dress. Unlike most fashion guides which typically tell you what's wrong and how to hide it, Elycia and Rita share how to love your figure and look fabulous doing it. I have worked with many wardrobe people who could learn a lot from this book. (Maybe if they read it, they wouldn't throw their hands up and roll their eyes while saying they don't know how to dress me!)

Many of us have run into some snooty salesperson at a clothing store who offers very little help. Even I've had my share of "Pretty Woman" moments where someone has made me feel self-conscious while shopping. This book will help you feel confident in your choices so you won't have the experience of feeling too scared to try something on that you love—or even worse, getting talked into buying a boxy cover-up that you'll never wear (and shouldn't).

Hiding your flaws is the wrong way to approach fashion. Getting dressed and looking fabulous should be fun, not stressful. Everyone's body is different, the trick is finding what works best for you.

Don't get me wrong, sometimes it takes three people to zip me up, but once it gets past my hips I look and feel amazing and it's always worth it!

————

Feminine, fearless, and oh so fabulous, Marissa Jaret Winokur rocks on every level. She floored audiences with her Tony Award-winning role as Tracy Turn-blad in the Broadway hit, Hairspray . . . *proved that she can shake and salsa with the best of them on* Dancing With The Stars . . . *and inspires women everywhere with her infectious enthusiasm and undeniable confidence. Marissa, you rule!*

ACKNOWLEDGMENTS

We'd like to thank our families who inspire and love us in all our endeavors . . . Edward and Naoko for creating such sexy, sassy visuals . . . Taura, for the stellar creative contributions . . . the always foxy Heather for the photo help . . . our fearless fabulous femmes, Amy K, Amy R, Barbara, Britt, Deena, Maya, Michaela, Raven, Taura, Tracey, Yasmine . . . Jane for her rockin' research . . . Tania Russell of Makeup Werks/ Nars for making everyone look so gorgeous . . . Al Zuckerman at Writers House for always believing in us . . . Marissa Jaret Winokur, Lisa Perkins, Steve "Cojo" Cojocani, Bonnie Fuller and Susan Kaufman for their support . . . and all the folks at Kensington/Citadel for their encouragement and ideas. A very huge and special thanks to our champion, Danielle Chiotti, whose passion for this project motivated us all the way through.

Curves Rule
and
Flat Is Fabulous

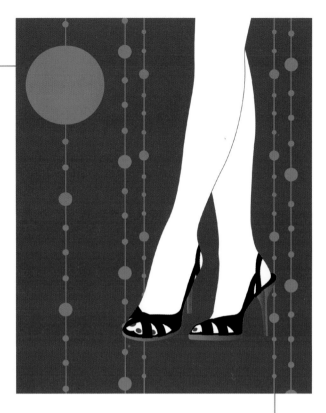

CHAPTER ONE

Got It, Flaunt It!

W e've all heard the same rants before: Don't wear wrap tops if you're flat. Don't wear capri pants if you're short. Don't wear slim jeans if you have hips. Don't do this, don't do that . . . who made up all of these rigid rules? Fashion should be fun, not bossy and formulaic.

The glossy fashion mags like to brand us into a certain "figure flaw" category, and suddenly we start looking at our body and clothes with dread. How's a girl supposed to know if she's an "hourglass" or an "inverted triangle"? What if you're a combination of several—and what the heck is an inverted triangle, anyway? Before you spiral into a bout of wardrobe depression and feel forced to donate your favorite jeans to Goodwill because they're not on the recommended list of fashion dos for your build, it may just be time for a fresh perspective.

Getting dressed shouldn't be about trying to cover up your boobs in a three-times-too-big blouse or hiding your rear under a shiny rayon bubble skirt. We say, work your womanly wiles, whether it's your bountiful breasts, shapely legs, or barely there butt. Go ahead, wear what you want and own your style—the trick is how you piece it all together. Our motto is, "It's not what you wear, it's how you pair!"

It's time to bust out of those forced fashion rules. And, we're not talking about spending a fortune, either. Flattering your figure is a cinch, no matter what your budget. Whether you're an athletic A-cup, curvy glamour queen, or five-foot fox—*Curves Rule and Flat Is Fabulous* shares how to flaunt your figure instead of letting it limit your style. Oh, and since we're big fans of keeping things simple, the variety of looks we share in this book are classics—the stuff that will endure; not overly trendy styles that are just a little too hip for the room.

So all you so-called pear shaped gals—peel away the layers! You "inverted triangles"—turn those fashion faux pas upside down! You booty queens, buxom divas, and flat-as-a-board femmes, redefine *style* according to your own rules. And never peek inside your closet with angst again!

BODY TYPE, SHMODY TYPE

Not everyone fits into the cookie-cutter body types ("pear," "boyish", and so on) that the majority of magazines and style guides recognize—and in fact, many of today's women don't fall into these specific categories at all. Our bodies are a collection of boobs, butts, shoulders, and tummies—which may be flat, full, long, short, ripped, robust, or any combination. So the idea that we can fit our feminine forms into just one of a handful of "types" starts to feel kind of fruitless.

In this book, we've defined women's shapes a bit differently—by putting more focus on body *parts*—you may be buxom and skinny, buxom and curvy, buxom and tall, or buxom and tiny. Each combination requires different strategies and techniques for dressing. We believe that women should feel comfortable and proud of their bodies—whatever you've got and wherever you've got it, flaunt it. And most important, flatter it!

No one wants to be crammed into a fashion box. So the how-to's for this book are boiled down to the basics. Figure out the combination of upper and lower body shapes that work best for you (for instance, you may be a Busty on top and Leggy on bottom with a hint of Booty thrown in). Then find your favorite styles, from boot-cut jeans to A-line skirts (like we said, you won't find a lot of "runway-inspired" or overly trendy items here . . . instead, we focus on key pieces that are timeless, effortless, and oh so alluring). That's it—the ultimate mix-and-match style system.

To get started, here's a quick intro of how we lovingly describe different types of foxy-figured women—mix and match to suit your body!

Booties

Boasting a full booty has become one of today's "most wanted" assets (pun intended). Curve-conscious clothing is designed to show off your sexiness. So ditch your baggies and work that rump!

Hipsters

The '50s screen sirens got it right—full-bodied and feminine, they really knew how to turn heads by flaunting their bodacious hips. They even named a song after you, so live it up, "Brickhouse"!

Belly Babes

It doesn't matter what endearing nickname you call it— pooch, tum-tum, or jelly. A belly with extra padding can be ultrafeminine (plenty of men agree!). And many of today's clothing styles are designed with that extra somethin' in mind, so wear every inch of that extra somethin' you have with pride!

Curvies

Lucky ladies who are deliciously curvaceous all over have a lot to work with. From boobs to booty, arms to abs, enjoy your full and quintessentially female shape. There's a lot to flaunt—now that's what we call a real plus!

Leggies

We haven't met a woman alive who wouldn't kill for a pair of glamorous gams. Although long, luxurious legs may come with their own special set of challenges for the five foot nine and over crowd, you can consider it more of a champagne problem: the rest of us say, "Cheers!"

Dainties

Sassy divas from Eva Longoria to Reese Witherspoon have discovered the secret to working small and stylish looks. Whether you're slim or curvy, those perfectly petite builds are the bomb.

Busties

Many women pay a lot of money to get what you've got. At the same time, we know all too well that being well endowed has its own hurdles, especially when it comes to finding a bathing suit top or bra that actually covers the full breast, not one quarter of it! With the right style savvy, you can do right by your D(+++) cups and look downright dishy!

Tatas

You're the envy of many, since you can wear just about any top, from skimpy halters to low-cut V's and triangle bikinis. If you're the proud owner of sweet, small boobies (a.k.a. tatas), take your pick and remember . . . flat is fabulous!

Broads

They invented shoulder pads to mimic what you've got. Sculpted shoulders are one of the most alluring features a woman can flaunt. Whether sexing it up in a sultry off-the-shoulder number or kicking back in a summery tank top, you're one stylish Broad!

MEET OUR FABULOUS FEMMES

There's nothing more enlightening than getting tried-and-true fashion tips from other women. Although we love browsing through the fashion favorites of celebs, or the picks of style editors in magazines, what we really crave is the advice of gals who are facing the same challenges that we are. So we gathered the sexiest and sassiest women we know and asked them to show us their most flattering outfits and best fashion tips. They come in all shapes and sizes, and each of them has an incredible sense of self *and* sense of style. Feeling comfortable in your skin is something no amount of money or designer paraphernalia can buy. These girls are fabulous for lots of reasons—because they embrace their curves, bust, and booty—because they have learned what makes them look and feel their best—and most of all, because they are truly beautiful (and sexy!) from the inside out. Meet our Fabulous Femmes.

Amy

Tracey

Deena

Britt

Barb

Maya

Raven

Yasmine

Michaela

Taura

Amy

CHAPTER TWO

Casual: Jeans and Tops

*I*t doesn't matter how many designer dresses make it onto every fashion editor's "It" list, how many sequin-slathered starlets prance down the red carpet, or how many glossy images of couture-clad models appear in monthly magazines . . . the favorite outfit for many modern-day women is still jeans and a top. But obviously we're not talking a hole-ridden pair of dungarees and a baggy T-shirt that boasts "San Antonio Spring Break '97" across the front.

How you wear and pair your denim makes the difference between dressing like a dud and looking like a diva. But without the right tips and tools, many women are left feeling like they have a better chance of walking down the aisle with George Clooney than finding a truly flattering pair of jeans. We endure hours of torture in the dressing room only to end up with a pile of misfits: like those "true-size" 29's that won't even budge an inch past our rump. Never mind the endless supply of trendy styles that come and go—light wash, dark wash, skinny-leg, wide-leg, high waist, beads, baubles— how's a girl supposed to keep up with it all?!

Still, have a little faith, feeling good in your favorite style of jeans is easier than you may think. There's a reason jeans are the uniform du jour for women from fourteen to fifty. If they're styled right, jeans are everything we want them to be—classic, casual, sexy, sassy, hip, and comfy.

Jeans and tops . . . Love 'em. Every inch of your bod, from your booty to your belly, can look better than you ever imagined just by pairing the best cuts for your shape with the most flattery-inducing tops and shoes.

Zip up a pair of sassy boot-legs; slip on a sheer, sexy top; and kick on some heels . . . your inner blue jean queen is ready to be unleashed.

Ladies, Start Your Denims

HALL OF FAME

Is there a pair of jeans that looks great on every woman? If we could invent them, we'd be billionaires! They just don't exist. We're not promising to make the mind-numbing denim hunt a breeze (yes, you could still find yourself in a dressing room up to your knees in jeans before striking the jackpot), but we will help narrow the search. Luckily, there are certain cuts that help to enhance *most* body types. And if we had to pick one universally flattering style for our Hall of Fame, it would be this: **fitted, long, low, dark, flared, and soft**.

- *Fitted.* We're not talking "I can't suck in an ounce of air" tight. Denim has come a long way . . . today's refined fabrics and modern cuts are designed to enhance (and *fit*) a woman's cushions and curves—from her waist to her hips and thighs. Never has there been a better time to boast some booty!

- *Long.* A longer cut lengthens the legs and gives a bit of slimming along the way (a little bonus most of us gals appreciate). Also, keep in mind what shoes you'll be pairing your jeans with—and allow for some heel. (Okay, *lots* of heel!)

- *Low.* A *slightly* lower-cut waist can work wonders, especially for those with a little belly. It makes jeans more comfy and helps to prevent a roly-poly midsection. But this is not a case of, "How low can you go?" Jeans that showcase your Hello Kitty skivvies (or worse yet, your glorious crack) just don't cut it.

- *Dark.* Dark washes are more sophisticated and classic than lighter washes (and yes, once again, slimming). Plus, tops and tees tend to pop more off darker tones, so your overall look will have more va-va-voom.

- *Flared.* A slightly flared leg gives any body shape a sexy silhouette. Whether you go for boot-leg or trouser-cut, a bit of feminine flare can balance out busty gals and give straighter bods a little curve.

- *Soft.* Jeans with a softer, thinner weave are more comfortable and less bulky feeling (and looking) than those made from thicker, stiffer fabrics. We remember the days when we had to wear our jeans for a year before they felt this cozy! Thankfully, today we have an endless array of options, so shop around for denims that are supple and have a bit of give.

FIT TO FLAUNT

Even the best-looking jeans may not feel right on your body if they aren't the proper size and style. Here's how to ensure a fabulous fit every time.

- Pick the right day to shop for jeans—in other words, *not* when you're in a foul mood, suffering from the breakup blues, having one of those inevitable "fat" days, or recovering from a record-setting Thanksgiving binge.

- It's a good idea to wear flip-flops for easy on-and-off. And bring an extra pair of heels and a few favorite tops to experiment with different looks.

- When trying on jeans, don't forget to move—sit, squat, spin, sit cross-legged, anything and everything to experience a full range of motion. Look for styles that offer a little give in the waist (but no thong-baring gaps!) as well as around the hips (without pulling and puckering). Jeans with a little stretch are usually much more comfy than the full-cotton styles and work wonders on every body type, especially full figures and Curvies. If you feel uncomfortable or stiff, then "take a pass" (as they say in Hollywood).

- Find a good tailor to nip and tuck where necessary—shortening the hem, adjusting the waistband, or getting rid of small bubbles of extra fabric. Basically, a trailor can make jeans look custom fit to your bod!

It's important to find a pro who knows how to alter a garment without drastically changing such fine details as belt loops or pocket placement. Just keep in mind that in general, you don't want to hem more than two inches since it may change the overall flare of the leg. Experienced tailors will ask whether you want a new hem put on the jean, or the existing hem sewn onto the adjusted length. Either way, find someone good to make you look good.

- Don't get frustrated by the mind-blowing price tags you find on many jeans. Great styles are available for every budget. We've found that the following lines have a little something for everyone and come at all different price points: Express, Target, Lucky Brand, Rock & Republic, Citizens of Humanity, Joes, J-Brand, and Gap. Another option, although a bit more costly, is Custom Levi's (you get to design your own style and fit from scratch).

JEANS 101

BOOT-CUT: With a slightly flared leg and hip attitude, boot-cut jeans never seem to go out of style. Why? Well, they're one of the most universally flattering styles—for everyone from Curvies to Dainties. As the name suggests, they look good with boots as well as chunky wedges and heels. If you only have room for one pair of jeans in your closet, this is it.

- *Booties and Hipsters:* Balance out your fuller booty with voluminous tops—trapeze-cut tees and ruffled blouses. Go for tops that hit at the hipline or slightly below. Another fun look is topping jeans off with a 3/4-length coat, to create a tailored silhouette. Boot-cut jeans will become your best friend—they're sassy and slimming. What more could we ask for!

- *Belly Babes:* Layering is a clever trick for a little dose of waistline slimming—wear a longer, stretchy tank peeking out from underneath a tee. For the most flattering look, try midrise to lower-cut styles that do not hit above the belly. If you're more comfortable wearing low-cut styles, pair them with long fluid or ruched tops to avoid the infamous "jelly roll."

- ***Leggies:*** Pair boot-cuts with longer tops that hit at the hip or just below—drawing the eyes away from the waist and giving you a lean, mean look. Play with sexy scoop necks or gauzy tunics. For those tall and *slender* figures (we'll try not to hate you), the slight flare of boot-cuts can actually create an illusion of curves. Pair them with tops that are structured at the waistline, such as a tapered silk blouse.

- ***Dainties:*** The trick for petite gals is to balance out the shapely curve of the boot-cuts with a form-fitting top, so you don't look overwhelmed by your clothes. Try hip-length V-neck tees with stretch, flutter-sleeve blouses, or spaghetti-strap tanks.

STRAIGHT-LEG: If you really want to crank up the foxy factor, slip on straight-leg jeans. This feminine style elongates the body and can be shortened without messing up the overall shape of the jeans (a big plus for Dainties). Pair them with high-heel boots or stilettos, for a sexy bonus.

- ***Booties and Hipsters:*** High or midrise cuts are best to support and flatter your shape and help ward off what is commonly called the "muffin-top" look. Pair these jeans with long, looser-fitting tops that drape and hit just below the hips—lightweight trapeze blouses, flared V-neck tunics, and draped tops with banded bottoms. Then slide into a pair of pointy-toe pumps.

- ***Belly Babes:*** Look for midrise jeans that hit across the belly, not above it. Choose a tank-style A-line blouse or ruched long-sleeve top that will compliment your fabulous tummy. Stick with soft or silky fabrics that won't cling to the skin, giving a more relaxed, comfortable fit.

- ***Leggies:*** Wear a long, lace-trimmed cami beneath a longer, loose-fitting sheer tee to create curves. Empire-waist tops and tunics are another stylish way to balance your shape. Complete the look with ballet flats or kitten heels.

- **Dainties:** These are perfect jeans for you—they'll help make your legs look longer and won't overwhelm your frame. Slip into stretchy, deep V-neck tops with gathering or details at the bust, along with a pair of pointy-toe flats. Add a long necklace to lengthen your look even more.

WIDE-LEG: A little bit groovy, a little bit rock and roll, wide-leg jeans come with a looser fit and a dash of funky attitude. This cut can be ultra-flattering for various shapes—and surprisingly, the wide leg will *not* make you look wider! You definitely want to wear heels, so pull out your wedges and mile-high peep-toes. And go with slim, feminine tops—your best bet for a look that is stylish, not sloppy.

- **Booties and Hipsters:** Curvy girls can really turn it out by pairing wide-legs with a stretchy wrap-style shirt to create an hourglass shape. Look for shirts that hit at the middle or lower part of the hip. Fitted jackets with flared hems also help to play up the waistline—slip one on over a satin tank and finish off your ensemble with a pair of shapely pumps.

- **Belly Babes:** Worn with a hip-length empire-waist top, these jeans will flatter your curves. A flowing fabric flares perfectly over the tummy to balance your bod in all the right places. Slip on peep-toe shoes to complete the look.

- **Leggies:** Pair these with a hip-length top—an off-the-shoulder top or boatneck tee—and Mary Janes or other feminine, round-toe flats for a clean, modern appearance.

- **Dainties:** Petite gals will likely have to alter their wide-leg jeans—but this style generally has a hemline that's easy to take up. Pair them with a sexy, fitted button-down that hits just at the hips and wedge shoes for a bit of additional height.

SLIM-CUT: Many of us feel there's a "slim" chance we could ever pull this style off, but when done right, it's a look that rates high on the sexy scale. Although the cut of these jeans might seem to flatter more long-and-lean silhouettes, those of us with extra padding can sport "skinnies" by accessorizing and balancing the look. In general, slim-cuts tend to work best with longer, looser tops. And whatever your shape, summon your inner goddess and pair your slims with devastating pumps.

- ***Booties and Hipsters:*** Slip on a fluid top with a flared trapeze or empire style that hits at the top of your thighs or slightly lower (at the widest part of your hips). And yes, some hiiiiiigh heels!

- ***Belly Babes:*** Pair slim styles with longer tops that are ruched on the sides; tees designed with fluid, non clingy fabrics (such as Micro Modal, Supima cotton, or cotton/nylon blends), or baby doll blouses. Then slip into strappy sandals and go.

- ***Leggies:*** These jeans look their best when balanced by a top that is full and long, so look for styles with volume, such as bell sleeves or unstructured, belted tunics. Leggy and lean gals who want to create an illusion of curves will love these tapered cuts, since they accentuate the hips. Finish off the look by tucking your skinny jeans into a pair of knee-high boots.

- ***Dainties:*** Slimmer cuts are a best bet for petite frames. Pair your slim jeans with a lace cami peaking out underneath a deep V-neck, along with kitten heel or pointy-toe pumps to help elongate your legs.

Pick Your Pocket

The size and placement of pockets is a huge factor in foxifying your fanny. Pockets should be proportionate to the size of your tush: not too big (which would hide your bottom) and not too small (which would exaggerate it). The higher pockets are, the more they tend to give your derriere a little lift. The lower, the more they tend to drag your bottom down and shorten the look of your legs.

TROUSER-CUT: Kick up the sophistication with this tailored and utterly feminine style. These jeans are polished and yet can also give you just a hint of femme fatale. They have a fuller leg, similar to wide-leg jeans, but the sassy difference is in the refined trouser styling and pocket design. Who knew "trousers" could look this good? We have to thank the men in our lives for donating a bit of masculine styling to give us a purely feminine feel.

- *Booties and Hipsters:* Look for a slimming dark wash, along with silky hip-length button-down blouses that are tapered at the waist and slightly flared toward the hem. To dress up your jeans, try a lacy cami underneath a belted wrap top with a flared hem. High-heel boots or wedges complete the look. If the front pockets happen to puff or pull, they can overaccentuate the hip area, so just have them nipped and tucked at your local tailor.

- *Belly Babes:* The trouser cut is a perfect match for Belly Babes, since they usually have a lower-cut waist. Play with girly button-downs that have funky or feminine detailing at midhip.

- *Leggies:* For a cool and classic look, pair trousers with untucked button-down tops that fall to the hipline and, depending on your mood, a flirty pair of kitten heels or simple flats.

- *Dainties:* Pair these jeans with a V-neck 3/4-length-sleeve tee that hits midhip . . . or a sweet cami layered underneath a fitted cardigan. Add peep-toe heels for extra height and sass.

Mamma Mia!

Maternity jeans can be a great option, even if you're not pregnant! Don't be shy about browsing through the "preggie" section of your local store to see what styles they have. For Belly Babes, Booties, and those who just want to be able to actually *breathe* in their jeans, maternity styles with those soft, stretchy, cotton waistbands can be ultra-flattering and supercomfy.

You're the Tops!

HALL OF FAME

From tees and tunics to curve-hugging blouses and sexy draped numbers, tops are one of the easiest ways to mix up and maximize your wardrobe. In the overall scheme of things, perfect-fitting tops are probably easier (or at least less frustrating) to find than pants, skirts, and such. But it's by no means a slam dunk! A top has to fit your shoulders without pulling, your boobs without puckering, your belly without bulging. But when you find that *one* that lifts and holds and fits and flatters, you're golden. Tops are the chewy nougat center of fashion—the place to have fun, add personality, play with color, and take a few chances. If we had to pick one universally flattering top for our Hall of Fame, it would be this: **long, sleeved, untucked, colorful, supportive, fluid, and V-neck**.

- *Long.* Look for tees and tops that hit midhip or below—flattering because they elongate your body and deemphasize the belly (when needed).

- *Sleeved.* Three-quarter- or elbow-length or long sleeves make the most of your shoulders and arms, and flatter everything from bony shoulders to back-of-the-arm wiggles.

- *Untucked.* From tees to button-downs, we prefer wearing tops untucked. Tucking tends to cut your body in half and can create unwanted bulges around the hips (who needs that?). On the other hand untucked styles lengthen and create one straight, fluid line.

- *Colorful.* Jewel tones and deep earth shades enhance all different skin tones and help brighten your best feature, your face! And for those who want to cheat off a few pounds, darker colors are always more slimming.

- *Support.* It doesn't matter how showstopping a top is if your boobs are dragging and drooping. Wearing a bra or camisole with built-in support underneath is a must. Ensure that your adorable A's and daring DD's look their absolute best!

- *Fluid.* Fabrics with a bit of give tend to accentuate the positive by hugging in all the right places. Look for smooth, medium-weight, cozy cottons, silks, and blends that provide sufficient coverage but don't get stiff or wrinkly. The fabric should fall smoothly over curves instead of clinging—just keep in mind that when the fabric is *too* thin, it can sometimes detail every bump, lump, and bulge in your glorious bod.

- ***V-neck.*** This is the single-most flattering neckline style. Every woman looks good in a V because it helps make the neck appear longer. In our book, the V stands for va-va-voom!

FIT TO FLAUNT

A fabulous top comes down to four things: how it drapes your shoulders, neck, chest, and tummy. And though some tops are designed to fit loose, we just want to make sure they don't look sloppy.

- Tops should fit around the shoulders without pulling or restricting your movement, around the chest without puckering or popping a button, and around the stomach without clinging. A great-fitting top should hang naturally and hit at about midhip. If it's too tight in any one area, move on.

- Don't just wear a bra—wear the right bra! That means one that camouflages your nips and gives you the desired amount of support (and cleavage!). If you want your bra straps to peek out deliberately, then make sure your undergarment is worthy of being out in public. No frayed, soiled straps and no white or beige (which tends to look like "underwear" instead of "lingerie"). Stick with dark colors, such as brown, black, navy, or racy red.

- Always check the front and rear view to ensure that a top flatters you from all sides. You want to make sure it compliments your boobs and belly, but also look at how it hugs or hangs around your booty, for the most ideal fit.

- When trying on new tops, bend down and touch your toes. Discover how much boob you may (intentionally or unintentionally) bare when you lean over. A subtle show of cleavage can be the sexiest thing on earth; just make sure you flash with finesse!

- Look for forgiving and figure-loving fabrics. Our all-time favorites: cotton and cotton Lycra blends.

TOPS 101

TEES: Whether V, scoop, round or crew neck, they're a staple in every girl's closet. Tees enjoy a glowing reputation as one of fashion's most user-friendly items. Although finding a flattering tee may sound easy, subtle variations in styles can take your look from nothing special to knockout in no time. Go ahead, fill your closet with tees in all types of shapes and shades—and flaunt a little T and A (a tee and attitude, that is)!

- **Busties:** Hip-length fitted tees with V- or cowl necks are a great match for Busties. They help to create a downward line on your bod, rather than widening it. V-necks are an easy choice because they allow for a little peek of cleavage (if desired) and break up your chest so it doesn't look overly imposing. Layer a 3/4-length-sleeve tee over a strappy tank in a contrasting color. Or mix it up with a small-print cotton cami underneath and solid Henley-style (button-placketed) tee with flared sleeves on top.

- **Tatas:** Tatas aren't limited in their tee choices—they can wear just about anything. Higher scoop-necks and V-necks, along with boatnecks, broaden the shoulder line and cheat the look of a slightly bigger bust. If, instead, you want to further enhance your boobs, try a sleeveless, flutter- or short-sleeve tee which focuses on the biggest part of your bust and gives you some extra oomph.

- **Belly Babes:** Slip into an empire-waist tee that is cinched just under the boobs, for a slim silhouette and flattering bust and tummy. Banded-bottom tees and high scoop-necks that drape slightly around the midsection are also great choices. Ruched tees (gathered along the sides and belly to create mini pleats) also work wonders to flatter the extra bit of lovin'!

- **Broads:** Pair jeans with V-neck tees to flatter the shoulder line and pull the eye downward. A feminine tank layered underneath a fluid Henley-style tee is the ideal way to soften and stylize your look. Once again, longer cuts will create a lean, luscious line and even out all your proportions.

TUNICS: They're comfy and sexy with a touch of bohemian flavor. But what we love most about tunics is that they're flattering and forgiving. And they easily transition from day to night . . . need we say more?

- *Busties:* Busties should choose a lower, slit-style neckline to show off a bit of collarbone and hint of cleavage. Definitely seek out styles that cinch in at the waist and flare at the hemline so that you don't lose your girly shape.

- *Tatas:* Tunics and Tatas are a match made in fashion heaven! Belted styles that tie under the bustline can give your boobs an extra half-cup of size. Flowing or flared sleeves also help to enhance your upper bod. And Tatas can experiment with patterns as well—look for tunics with a little 'tude.

- *Belly Babes:* Belly Babes will want to live in tunics once they try them. Look for styles that are tailored just slightly at the waist and then flare downward. Slip on a simple embroidered tunic over a slim pair of jeans or leggings and finish it off with a pair of casual flats or flip-flops.

- *Broads:* Broads can look for long tunics that balance out the upper bod. Any kind of vertical design element (such as ties that hang, or beading) will also help to keep the look lean and fluid.

Let's Mention the Unmentionables!

Undies are the foundation pieces of a great look. The right bra provides lift, a bit more size, or just the right amount of cleavage. The right panties preserve the beauty of your booty without bubbles or bulges. The one basic wear-with-anything bra to consider for your wardrobe: a **silky, neutral, molded cup (with or without underwire).** When it comes to panties, it's all about the thong—a **low-cut meshy nylon or ultralight cotton** pair is invisible on every body shape. Fill out your lingerie drawer with specialty bras (halter, convertible, padded), slimmers and shapers (such as Spanx), and even maternity bras (which offer added support even when you're not expecting!).

BLOUSES: Of all the words in fashiondom, this one always tends to sound dated. It doesn't have the sizzle of *stiletto* or the sweetness of *sweater*. Instead, it reminds us a little too much of something Grandma would wear. We prefer to say *button-downs*. Okay, so they don't all have buttons . . . but you get the drift. Whatever you call them, just like with tees, every girl should stock her closet with them. From classic button-downs with a touch of stretch to gauzy girly numbers, blouses forever remain a feminine and flawless look.

- **Busties:** The vertical line of buttons helps balance out Busty bods beautifully. Well-endowed gals who have issues with buttons pulling and popping can buy a size larger and have the rest of the blouse tailored to fit . . . or wear a cami under the blouse and leave it partially unbuttoned. Styles with tiny prints and subtle textures, small collars, no pockets, and toned-down details are most flattering.

- **Tatas:** Fitted button-downs can be a Tata's best friend. Slip on a cute tank underneath (to add a little extra layer to the chest) and leave just one or two top buttons undone for a relaxed yet polished look. Blouses with ruffles, smocking, chest pockets, and wide collars can further amp up your boobs.

- **Belly Babes:** Belly Babes are stunning in button-downs that have a little stretch in the fabric, along with a feminine, tailored cut. Look for cuts that cinch in a bit right above the waistline and then flare out. Sheer swinging-cut blouses made from whispery lightweight cottons and silks are also ultra-flattering—layer over a cami for a great night-out look.

- **Broads:** Broads can work this style flawlessly. Keep it unbuttoned a bit lower to create a feminine look—sexy instead of stiff. Play with subtle vertical pinstripes or small patterns and textures for added interest. Tuxedo-style blouses are a great match for you as well.

SEXY DRAPED TOPS: Whether showing off silky shoulders, that defined (and divinely alluring) collarbone, or those beautiful breasts (large or small), we have a lot to flaunt. And our stash of sexy, draped tops helps us do just that. Blousy spaghetti straps, flowing numbers, and off-the-shoulder cuts will help make the most of your assets. The right fabric is key to getting a look that is truly sexy—fluid silks, sheer chiffons, and loose rayons are what it's all about. And the right foundation pieces are a must, too, so stock up on nude and black bras and camis.

- *Busties:* Slip into a draped V- or cowl neck to help soften the bustline and accentuate the upper body. Experiment with strapless bras or wear a cami with built-in support underneath satin or sheer styles. Convertible halter-style bras can also be a lifesaver with this alluring top.

- *Tatas:* These tops were made for you. The drapey styling helps accentuate a smaller chest. And you'll look your sexiest in sleeveless or off-the-shoulder cuts that draw attention to alluring assets such as shoulders and arms.

- *Belly Babes:* Perfect for concealing a tummy, silky flowing styles will show off your shoulder blades and back, and steer focus away from the belly. Look for flared off-the-shoulder pieces that are slightly cinched at the waist. Take full advantage of drapey fabrics such as buttery cotton jersey or silk charmeuse.

- *Broads:* Soft silky cowl necks or plunging necklines will flatter your shoulders in just the right way. Play up your décolletage with a bit of beading or sequins around the neck and bust.

––––––

WRAP TOPS: Wrap shirts should be a staple in every woman's wardrobe. They lift and define our boobs, shape our waist, love our tummy, and flatter our hips. We can find no fault! Hip-length styles work best on all different body types—and from there you can take your pick of long- or short-sleeve and even sleeveless wrap tops (which are not only summer necessities but can easily spice up any evening look year-round).

- **Busties:** The wrapped styling and sexy V-neck is ideal for you. As always, a supportive bra is essential. The plunging cut shows off just the

right amount of skin but doesn't leave you overexposed. If the V winds up falling a bit too low exposing more of you than you'd like, slip on a delicate lace cami underneath for added coverage.

- **Tatas:** Make the most of wrap tops by layering a colorful cami underneath and wearing styles where the V hits a bit higher up on the chest. Add a chunky necklace to enhance your upper bod and you're ready to go.

- **Belly Babes:** Wraps are perfect for Belly Babes since they define the waist, helping to create an hourglass look. Look for extra wrapping and gathering around the tummy for the most flattering fit.

- **Broads:** The natural V-neckline shifts the focus downward and brings attention toward the waist. Your best bet would be a dark, solid wrap shirt with ¾-length sleeves, helping to create a lean, feminine figure.

TANKS AND HALTERS: These are two sexy styles for showing off your upper body assets. We love wearing them alone during the warm-weather months or underneath fitted jackets. It's a look that demands support, especially for Busties, so remember to grab a halter-cut bra in the lingerie department.

- **Busties**: Look for V-neck halters to show off your killer cleavage. Another great option: halters that cut straight across—these will give you a bit more coverage. As for tanks, try pieces that are designed with thicker straps and cut higher up beneath the arm for added support.

- **Tatas:** Wide-set halter straps help create the illusion of a bigger chest. Styles with ruching around

The Wiggles

The Wiggles are those mysterious little flabs on the back of our arms (the area muscle-pumping guys call a "tricep"). Since most of us may not have hours to spend at the gym trying to tighten them up, we've come up with a few tricks. Among our favorites: 3/4-length-sleeve tees, elbow-length cashmere cardigans, and bell- or kimono-sleeved tunics . . . perfect for flattering those little somethings you haven't had the chance to work on just yet.

the bust will enhance the effect even more. Tank tops are ultra-flattering—try out styles embellished with beading or patterns, or made of thicker, textured fabrics to give some added oomph to your upper bod.

- *Belly Babes:* Halters are a great style for your shape—especially baby dolls. They cinch at the chest and drape downward, flattering the tummy. Stick with fabrics that have a bit of stretch and lay softly over the skin. Flared, empire-waist tanks with wider straps are another flattering option.

- *Broads:* The plunging neckline of halters balances broader shoulders and elongates your shape by drawing attention front and center. As for tanks, experiment with racer backs, which can flatter and feminize the line of your shoulders.

———

EMPIRE WAIST: This is a look that's drenched in femininity. When you want to flatter an extra bit of belly or amp up a small chest, head straight for this style. With a raised waistline that hits just below the bust, empire tops flatter long torsos because they camouflage the natural waistline, and short torsos because they lengthen the midsection. In other words, it's hard to go wrong. Since this tends to be a more voluminous look, empire waists often work best with more fitted bottoms. There's something easygoing and a bit bohemian about this style—top it off with a pair of wedges and a long, beaded necklace for an effortlessly sexy look.

- ***Busties:*** V-neck styles in soft, brushed cottons with ruching beneath the bust help create an hourglass shape. Kimono-style empire waists are especially flattering (on various body types) and we love them because the flared arms balance out bigger boobs. Busties should look for lower empire tops that sit below the boobs rather than cutting across them.

- ***Tatas:*** This is the ideal top for small busts, especially when it's fitted. The tight cinch under the bust will help make the breasts look bigger, creating a curvier figure. Sign us up! For a little extra punch, Tatas can try on styles that have extra detailing, such as belts or bows just under the boobs.

- ***Belly Babes:*** Empires are the Belly Babe's best buddy since they bring the focus to the chest, away from the belly. The high waistband completely hides the tummy, creating a sexy flow and curvy body shape. Stock up on 'em!

- ***Broads:*** Styles designed with daring V-necks and cinching at the bust will go a long way to enhance your shape. High-cut sleeves that are set in a bit on the shoulder will create a narrow line. You can also experiment with ribbed fabrics or vertical patterns that give the illusion of long lines—empire tops with ties that hang down can achieve the same effect.

FABULOUS FEMMES

Deena:

Pure Italian, from her dark locks to her sun-kissed olive skin, Deena is a Dainty who decks out her delicate frame in feminine pieces with funky, eclectic touches. "For years, I've been insisting that I must be built completely unlike anyone else . . . I'm curvy and petite, barely over five foot one. Of course, thanks to the three-inch heels I wear, I really consider myself to be more like five foot four!"

Jeans (always with heels) "are one of the most important staples in my closet," she says. She favors a mid-to-low waist with boot- or slim-cuts in darker rinses, which she says "tend to be most flattering."

Over the years, Deena has learned how to max out her petite frame. "I realized if I wore really high heels but kept my jeans as long as possible (so they just graze the floor), I could make my legs appear much longer than they really are, especially with a more fitted thigh and slight flare at the ankle. I do this with all of my pants, too . . . it's key for girls with short legs." Deena proves that you don't have to be built like a runway model to wear super-slim-cuts. "I especially like to wear them with heels and a tunic or sexy off-the-shoulder top that hits just below my hips to create one lean line. All of my slim jeans have a bit of stretch. I live in them!"

Britt:

Britt rocks. Literally. The only girl in the popular Los Angeles–based band Guilt by Association, she holds her own against the guys onstage and off. Blond, busty, and leggy (she stands five foot eleven), we love her laid-back style, which includes lots of jeans, layered tees or tanks, and Converse sneakers or flip-flops.

But finding the right jeans isn't so easy. "Let me describe my shopping nightmares: a tiny dressing room filled to the brim with jeans in any size from 8 to 12, because designers just aren't consistent. I also have to search for everything in long or extra long, which very few stores carry." Finding flattering tops can also be a challenge because of her athletic torso (her arms are buff from years of surfing). "For shirts to fit over my breasts and not squeeze too tight around my arms, I usually have to buy a size large, which makes the shirt stick out around my tummy with a very boxy look. To fix this, I usually choose a soft, stretchy material."

Among Britt's favorites are empire-waist tops. To avoid a blousy, tent effect, she looks for styles that sit low on her chest and accentuate her cleavage but "in a nontrashy way." Most flattering are hemlines that fall right at the middle of her tush, paired with fitted jeans. By pulling focus to her chest (not boobs) and shoulders and choosing a stream-lined bottom, she balances the flowing style of the shirt. "When I shop for clothes, the first things I check are my butt and my boobs. If they look good, then I will consider the rest. It can be challenging to find the right fit but when I do it is super cute!" We couldn't agree more. Rock on, Britt!

Barb:

Deliciously down-to-earth, Barb is a girl's girl through and through. This entrepreneurial mother of three loves to cook, so how apropos that she whipped up her very own line of homemade brown sugar body scrubs and lotions, which are now selling like hotcakes! Always on the go, Barb's everyday look is purely clean and classic. "I used to want to believe I was an 'hourglass,'" she says, "but whenever I tried to follow the 'rules,' I would end up looking goofy." After much experimenting, she now characterizes her figure as "athletic with a twist of femme fatale. I have a 'petite' torso and regular legs, broad shoulders, and a round rib cage that makes me appear larger in a side view."

Barb loves to pair modern, curve-hugging jeans with dark neutrals such as black and brown—and of course, an amazing pair of heels! "No matter what your height, jeans should be worn with heels—otherwise curvy can look dumpy." Since she has what she calls "a bit of a hook in the back," some jeans tend to have an unsightly gap there. To remedy the problem, she has her mother "toddlerize" them by opening the waistband and adding a six-inch nonrolling elastic band. "They look like toddler pants when they are not on your body, but they fit perfectly."

Barb never tucks in her tops and favors styles that fit her hips and waist—stretchy button-down blouses that are tailored at the waist, along with form-fitting crewneck, boatneck, and V-neck tees. Even in the simplest jeans and top, she's one hot mama!

Maya:

Artsy and beautiful with a bohemian flair, Maya glows without a stitch of makeup and has perfected the art of being super-comfy *and* stylish. Whether she's making an appearance at one of the hip boutiques that sell her line of jewelry, Maya Brenner Designs, or hitting the farmers' market with her kids, she is always pulled together in the most effortless way. When asked to describe her body, she says, "My figure now or before having two kids?!" Although motherhood may have blessed her with a little "flesh apron" on her tummy, her thin legs, curvy chest, and toned shoulders are her favorite spots to flaunt.

A native of California, Maya has been a jeans lover all her life. These days, she likes them "roomy in the hips, tighter on the legs, hitting right below the belly button. The best fitting pant—every time I wear them, everyone says that I look so skinny—are the 'Angel' cords by AG. Very tight in the legs, but roomier in the butt and waist." She pairs them with fluttery feminine blouses or structured cotton tops with lace or embroidered details . . . and usually a pretty-but-practical shoe, such as a modern clog or flip-flop. Who knew casual could look so irresistible!

CHAPTER THREE

Sophisticated: Pants and Jackets

It's hard to believe there was ever a day when women didn't wear pants! Then such Hollywood glamour girls as Greta Garbo and Katharine Hepburn burst onto the scene with their sexy swagger and changed the way women dressed forever. Talk about two fabulous femmes!

Pants and jackets are the tailored pieces that pump up our wardrobe and allow us to turn out sophisticated daytime looks, along with elegant evening ensembles. And we definitely couldn't survive at the office without them. Yet, when one says, "flawlessly feminine," the first image that comes to mind is probably not a woman in pants and a jacket. Paft of the reason: this is a look that can be tricky to pull off—ill-fitting pants can easily bunch or bulk, and it's a cinch to go from flawless to flunky when slipping on a boxy, shoulder-pad-laden jacket.

From wide-cuff slacks to wide-lapel blazers, here's the skinny on how to perfect the look of pants and jackets. Rethink how these staples can add new sizzle to your personal style, whether you're a working girl or just working it, girl!

Fancy Pants

HALL OF FAME

Our wardrobe would never be complete without them—pants. They can be feminine, funky, fierce, and completely frustrating! There's the age-old dilemma of finding a pair that fit in the tush but seem to gap and gape at the waist . . . or that fit your midsection to perfection but make your derriere look as if it's trying to break out and run for the hills. Why is it so hard to find pants that fit your female bod *everywhere*? And then there are so many complicated bells and whistles—zippers, buttons, belt loops, pockets, pleats, cuffs, and on and on.

Before you give up on pants and commit yourself to a diet of only dresses and skirts, try on our Hall of Fame for size. All figures, from Dainties to Leggies, will want to stock up on what we like to call "the perfect pant": **flat, flared, black, with simple pockets**.

- *Flat.* Whether you're flat as a board or sporting a little tummy, flat-front pants create a more streamlined look—with none of that icky bulging you get with pleats. The bottom line is: pleats just ain't pretty. If you want to look foxy, go with flat.

- *Flared.* Trends and tastes come and go, but slightly flared pants is a style that always endures. A little flare can look rock and roll (with a funky tee) or classic (with a sexy button-down)—and the shape works magic to balance out your body.

- *Black.* Black is the single gotta-have-it color. The dark tone (along with other neutrals such as navy and brown) will give you a long, lean look—plus, they never go out of style. Look for fabrics with a little stretch, such as gabardine/cotton blends—they're designed to hug you in all the right places and retain their shape.

- *Simple pockets.* The fancier pants' pockets, the more room for bunching and VPL (visible pocket lines). So keep it simple—slits in the rear or nothing at all. For Hipsters who feel that trouser-style side pockets can be the kiss of death, try small front pockets. We happen to love pocketless pants—they're simply sublime!

FIT TO FLAUNT

Whether you're shopping for everyday or evening, finding off-the-rack perfect-fitting pants can be a challenge (milelong hemlines, anyone?), so our number one tip is to have a tailor in your speed dial!

- Look for fabrics that can take some wear and tear *and* offer versatility, giving you the most bang for your buck. A dark, subtle pinstripe can be paired with a casual T-shirt for day and then dressed up with a sexy V-neck sweater for evening . . . and won't show every little speck of food or dirt that may come your way.

- The most classic hem length is one that barely skims the floor. Too long, and your pants will be collecting dust bunnies; too short, and you're "flooding." Which leads us to our next point . . .

- When shopping, take along two or three pairs of shoes to get a sense of how pants can be dressed up or down—literally. Flats, midheel boots, and high heels will cover it.

Off the Cuff

There's something about the swanky attitude of a cuff that keeps us interested. Leggies wear cuffs well, as the extra detail breaks up the leg line. Cuffs can also balance out Booties and Hipsters by adding some width and focus at the bottom. Pair with simple, streamlined tops so you don't have too much going on overall. A tweed cuffed trouser and autumn-hued cashmere V-neck is one of our favorite fall looks!

- Do the rear-view check. If you can see the outline of your panties underneath, it may be time to trade in those unlined slacks for a pair with a lining or thicker fabric. Ditto for any lovable rolls and dimples on the derriere—if anything feels a little too exposed, take a pass.

- Check to make sure the fit is cozy in the crotch. Not too snug, or the dreaded CT ("camel toe") will be on display with all of its unwanted glory; not too low, or it might look as if you're hiding something in there.

PANTS 101

FLARED: Flared-leg pants are universally flattering (after all, they were inducted into our Hall of Fame). Make them a staple in your closet and mix and match with a wardrobe of button-downs, barely there camis, and sophisticated tees, for an endless array of looks. Pants with a slight flare are versatile beyond belief—day, night, casual, dressy, sassy, summery . . . they're great with flats and gorgeous with heels. What more can we say?

- ***Booties and Hipsters:*** Pair your flares with flowing, loose-cut blouses and empire tops. Or try a dressy tank underneath a hip-length jacket that flares at the hem. Look for medium-or heavier-weight fabrics with just a bit of stretch—wool or cotton blends with Lycra for give.

- ***Belly Babes:*** Fall in love with low or midrise styles. And let your beautiful belly breathe a little! Complete the flattering look with layering on top—a tank top underneath a sheer or silky button-down that tapers in at the waist and flares to midhip. Or try a structured hip-length blazer that accentuates your waist and beautifies your belly area.

- ***Leggies:*** Long, shaped tees and V-neck sweaters pair perfectly with flared pants. Try layering a long top underneath a shorter bomber-or aviator-style jacket, for a lean, edgy vibe.

- ***Dainties:*** Go fitted on top, to keep your look balanced. A subtle patterned tee, gauzy printed cami, or silky tank underneath a tailored, hip-length blazer will create the perfect petite silhouette.

STRAIGHT: Classic and fitted, straight-leg pants have a sleek edge that we can't resist when paired with a flowing top and up-to-there pumps . . . or a cashmere V-neck and ankle boots. Don't underestimate them—they may be a bit more serious than flares or a little less funky than wide-legs, but straight-leg styles can be every bit as divine. Look for fabrics that stay crisp and unwrinkled—wool crepes, silk blends—and choose shoes with attitude, to give your straight legs a little sass.

- *Booties and Hipsters:* Larger back pockets and wide waistbands are good tricks to balance your bum. Look for styles with a lower-cut waist that won't annoyingly dig into the midsection. Pair with longer, contoured button-downs that flare out from the waist, or a 3/4-length jacket worn open over a fitted V-neck.

- *Belly Babes:* Anyone with a little extra lovin' in the tummy should look for flat-front styles that hit right below the belly button. Slip on a ruched button-down (with a bit of give in the fabric) or an empire-waist top; finish off with a pair of strappy high-heel sandals.

- *Leggies:* Balance your leggy bod by pairing straight-leg pants with a long, boatneck sweater or hip-length tee layered under a cropped jacket. Finish off with a pair of embellished flats or sexy kitten heels.

- *Dainties:* Straight legs are a smart style for Dainties, as they help to elongate your silhouette. Pair them with a deep V-neck sweater and high-heel boots (remember, the hem should be kept long—just skimming the floor) for a supremely seductive look.

WIDE-LEG: Wide-leg styles are loaded with attitude . . . not to mention those useful little perks—the cut helps to lengthen and slenderize. Everyone from Hipsters to Dainties can step out in this flowing style. Pair them with a fitted top (to balance the fluid bottom) and heels to really make a statement!

- *Booties and Hipsters:* Curvy girls, this style is a definite keeper for you. The long hem and roomier cut are ultra-flattering to your silhouette. If you haven't already filled your closet with this style, start making room. Wide legs are especially alluring when coupled with a hip-length scoop-neck sweater, cool necklace, and wedges.

  - *Belly Babes:* Wide legs give Belly Babes an easy way to flatter and add some flair to their wardrobe. Work them with a flutter-sleeve, empire-waist top or a long-sleeve, stretchy, ruched one. Or try layering a camisole underneath a fitted wrap sweater. Look for tops that hit on the hip.

  - *Leggies:* Try wide-leg styles with big cuffs at the bottom and match with a long, boatneck tee and a wide belt worn low on the hips—this evens out your proportions. Slip on a pair of wedges or funky flats to complete the look and go!

  - *Dainties:* Wide legs should fit a bit more snugly in the hips and tush, so you aren't swimming in them. Stick with body-hugging tops such as stretchy button-downs, V-neck tees, and halters. And of course, kick it up with strappy heels or mile-high vintage-inspired peep-toes.

CAPRIS AND CROPPED: With a nod to old Hollywood, we always envision Audrey Hepburn scooting around the Italian island of Capri on a Vespa, on her way to lunch at some charming little seaside bistro. There is an army of women who think any pant that is "tapered" is just plain evil (and sometimes, we agree), but the shorter styling (ending at midcalf) gives these pants a carefree vibe that works equally well with a summery sweater and flats or a long tee and flip-flops. Wear capri pants right and you'll be swearing by them soon enough.

- **Booties and Hipsters:** Capris designed with a slight flare at the bottom will help draw attention to the bottom half of the leg. Stick with darker colors, such as brown and navy, and pair them with a relaxed linen button-down (roll up the sleeves for casual flair) or a vibrant empire-waist tunic.

- **Belly Babes:** The flat-front styling is a flattering fit for Belly Babes—as always, look for midrise cuts that are comfy on the tummy. Banded-bottom tops or easy, breezy tees that are slightly loose fitting will pair perfectly with this look. And don't forget some colorful sandals.

- **Leggies:** Cropped styles are a smart pick for gals with long legs. Hip-length wrap shirts, summery V-neck sweaters, or soft, carefree linen button downs, along with ballet flats, finish off this classic look.

- **Dainties:** Although petites are often told to swear off capris, this is a fresh look that you can easily pull off. Tapered styles are the most flattering. We love them with flowing chiffon tops, long tanks (you can add a lightweight cropped cardigan on top), or hip-length halters. Top if off with a *sexy* wedge.

CARGOS: With their funky, playful styling and loose, comfy fit, cargos have become a casual wardrobe staple. We like to keep it simple with these pants by choosing styles that don't OD on pockets, drawstrings, zippers, and all those other extras. Slip on your cargos as a casual alternative to jeans—you may just want to live in them all weekend long.

- **Booties and Hipsters:** You'll like the sassy, looser-fitting style, especially when you get a peek at how great your rear view looks! Your best bet are cargos with minimal pockets placed a bit lower on the thigh. Pair with a fitted hip-length V-neck sweater or tee and your favorite pair of sneakers.

- **Belly Babes:** What could be better than cargos with a nifty drawstring waist that lets you make them as fitted or roomy as your belly is in the mood for. Slip on a fluid, hip-length, boatneck tee and flip-flops, and you're ready for some fun in the sun.

- *Leggies:* The looser line and added pockets of cargos will give nice shape to the lower half of your body. And your long, gorgeous legs help make these casual pants look extra lean and refined. Create a relaxed, cozy look with a couple of long, fitted layered tees and colorful simple slides for added kick.

- *Dainties:* Petite frames can do well with more refined cargo styles. Stick with slightly tapered cuts and wear them with a short-sleeve button-down and an espadrille wedge.

————

EVENING: Who doesn't love an opportunity to pull out those "special occasion" clothes? Whether we're headed to a cocktail gathering or fund raiser, we love to parade our fancy pants—silky slacks, feminine tuxedo styles, and sumptuous velvets are among our favorites. Polish the look off with a sexy after-hours top, pair of dressy sandals, and a satin clutch. The night is yours!

- *Booties and Hipsters:* Step out in wide-leg crepe or silk-blend pants. Dark, classic tones such as black and chocolate brown are slimming and sexy. Couple them with a silky, hip-length ivory button-down—go low-cut for a bit of drama, and dress up the style with a flared collar or dramatic sleeves. Finish with a pendant necklace and colorful bag.

- *Belly Babes:* Toast the town in flared, flat-front satin or stretchy gabardine styles with a wider-cut waistband. An elegant empire-waist top or slightly sheer, collared button-down that flares at the waist (worn over a cami) completes the look. Other feminine details such as pin tucks or small ruffles will also dress it up. The final touch; a few bangles or a wide cuff bracelet.

- *Leggies:* Leggies were born to prove just how ultrafeminine pants can be! Make a statement in silky, sleek trouser styles that are fitted in the hips and waist and slightly flared from the tops of the thighs. Pair them with a sophisticated and sexy halter . . . or a low-cut tailored evening jacket with a sexy lace camisole peeking out. Add a bit of bling with delicate drop earrings.

- ***Dainties:*** Low-waist, straight-leg tuxedo styles with stripes down the side can elongate your figure especially when paired with a shrunken blazer. Velvet pants are a real wow on petite frames, as well—stick with styles that are snug at the top and have a slight flare starting at the knee. Off-the-shoulder tops or delicate camis worn underneath cropped cashmere cardigans will dress up the look to perfection.

From Bombers to Blazers . . .

HALL OF FAME

Just like the cherry on top, jackets complete any look. They can also take a so-so ensemble to so spectacular. With such a wide variety of cuts, styles, and fabrics, jackets maximize your wardrobe and instantly transform any outfit—they can make you look tough, feminine, vampy, sporty, edgy, or sophisticated. They're also one of the most versatile pieces in your closet. Pair them with pants, dresses, jeans, or skirts, to whip up your own personalized look. The trick is finding a jacket that doesn't tug at the shoulders and beneath the arms, and won't pull and pucker at the bust and belly. Be prepared to try on several of them before landing a winner, but narrow your search by giving our favorite style a whirl: **mid-hip, 1 to 2 buttons, moderate lapel, low-cut, feminine styling, and black**.

- ***Mid-hip.*** It's one of the most modern cuts around—a jacket that falls to midhip. Not too long, not too short—it flatters every area from your belly to butt.

- ***1 to 2 buttons.*** Keep it simple with just one or two buttons. You want a jacket to drape stylishly rather than feeling stiff and "all buttoned up." The more buttons, the more fussy and conservative a jacket tends to look, so less is more here.

- ***Moderate lapel.*** Too wide and you'll be feeling that '70s fever complete with disco balls. A moderate lapel is timeless and works well with a variety of looks.

- ***Low-cut.*** Nothing's sultrier than a low-cut jacket. Whether you layer it over a stretchy silk tank, flowy cami, or sexy button-down, you want your jacket to show just a little somethin'.

- *Feminine styling.* Look for simple blazer styling with a feminine twist—tailored close to the body to flatter your silhouette around the boobs and waist, and with a slight flare toward the hem to accentuate your hips in all the right ways. Be sure the arms are slim and fitted (while still allowing comfy movement), and stick with minimal pads (or none at all) to show off those sassy shoulders.

- *Black.* Every closet yearns for one—a go-anywhere, wear-with-anything black jacket. It never goes out of style and works just as well with jeans as it does with dressy ivory dinner slacks.

FIT TO FLAUNT

Jackets come in so many shapes and styles that the idea of "fit" starts to make your head spin. Sleeves and shoulders can be a problem area for some, but with the right tricks up those sleeves, trying on jackets will be a bit easier.

- The right jacket should show your curves, not hide them, so slightly fitted and not too boxy is what we're going for. Key areas to check are shoulders, breast, and belly. If any of these is too small, then pass—there's little a tailor can do to make it work. A jacket should hug your shoulders without puckering, skim your torso without pulling, and fall over your bottom without bulging. It may just need a little nip and tuck to tighten the shoulders or perhaps shorten the sleeves.

- Do the arm check: raise them up in the air and stretch them out to make sure the jacket doesn't tug under your arms. It doesn't matter how ridicu-

---

Suit Up

A timeless black pantsuit in a rich fabric such as gabardine, brushed cotton, or silk blends is a must and works for all shapes. Stick with classic styling—a one-or two-button jacket that hits midhip and has a sophisticated lapel, and flat-front pants with a slight flare. Look for subtle feminine touches—a slight flare to the jacket hem or a shaped lapel.

lous you feel doing the Chicken Dance in the dressing room mirror, this is the best way to figure out if the fit is right.

- If you're planning on wearing a thicker or bulkier top underneath, try one on with the jacket to make sure the fit still works and the arms don't feel too tight and binding. Even if you can't close all of the buttons, the jacket may still look sleek worn open. Give it a whirl!

- Think about what you're going to wear with a new jacket. There's nothing worse than falling in love with a cool leather bomber or sassy tweed blazer only to get home and find out you really have nothing to pair it with. And since jackets can be a higher-ticket item, look for styles that can be worn day or night, dressed up or down, and transitioned from season to season.

JACKETS 101

HIP-LENGTH: Crank up your foxiness with the modern styling of this jacket. Dress it up with flat-front pants, a silky button-down, and sky-high pumps, or create a more relaxed look by pairing it with jeans, a funky tee, and colorful flats.

- *Belly Babes:* You'll look your best in styles that are cinched above the waist to give some added definition. Experiment with buttonless or single-button styles that offer a comfy fit. Wear this jacket over a flowing blouse that hangs out underneath, to soften your tum.

- *Busties:* For you, one-button, single-breasted, low V-neck cuts are best. Look for styles with small to moderate lapels that flatter without overwhelming your upper bod.

- *Booties and Hipsters:* A truly feminine cut that fits through the boobs and waist and that flares out over the hips will give all your curves some kick. Pair with a silky scoop-neck tank or light, patterned, flutter-sleeve blouse.

- *Dainties:* Shop for fitted, shrunken-style jackets with tapered or ¾-length sleeves and play around with layered looks. Slip on a body-skimming baby doll top or long V-neck tee that just peeks out from underneath. It's an alluring look without overwhelming your shape.

———

LONG: When you're in the mood for something that ranks high in sophistication, this is the jacket. Keep it tailored so that the fabric falls close to the body, accenting your lovely silhouette. Since this is a lengthier cut, it looks best when worn with pants or jeans. It's a versatile style you can dress up for elegant cocktail and dinner parties, play a bit more conservative for on the job, or funk up with a dose of downtown attitude for casual nights out.

- **Belly Babes:** Streamlined jackets work well for you—collarless and buttonless cuts offer a clean, modern line that complements your curves. A slightly tapered waist and un-boxy fit is key. Try ¾-length or long sleeves scrunched up to the elbow if you want to loosen up the look. Single-button styles that close above the waist are another great bet and can be worn open as well. Slip one on with wide-leg pants; a long, feminine, spaghetti-strap tank or scoop-neck sweater; and a bold necklace.

- *Busties:* Step out in jackets with understated lapels that can be worn open. When you are looking for a little "closure," try one-button styles that hit mid-abdomen since they won't tighten and tug. Depending on how much you want to flaunt what you've got, slip on a silky scoop-neck tank or sleek turtleneck (yes, you can wear t-necks!) and sassy trousers.

- *Booties and Hipsters:* A tapered waist will give your shape some wow—look for styles that accentuate your midsection and then flare toward the hem. Try with boot-cut jeans, a fluid V-neck sweater and sky-high boots . . . or flared, flat-front pants, an empire-waist top and pointy-toe pumps.

- *Dainties:* Look for jackets with defined shoulders—a bit of *subtle* padding can enhance your upper body. Narrow lapels are also a best bet, since they create a balanced, modern line. Add slim pants, a body-skimming blouse, and feminine wedges, and you're delicious, Dainties!

––––––––

LEATHER AND SUEDE: Loaded with a megadose of sexy attitude, leather and suede jackets just seem to exude confidence. It's a look that tends toward the edgy, especially when you pair a sleek, fitted cut with jeans and boots. But we also love surprising combos, such as a leather bomber over a flirty dress, or a suede jacket with evening pants and a silk cami. Because these items can be a bit pricey, look for classic cuts and colors that can work wonders with different pieces of your wardrobe. And remember, leather doesn't just have to feel hard core—it can be superseductive and girly!

- *Belly Babes:* Collarless open-style leather and suede jackets (with or without a zipper) create a clean, cool vibe without the binding feel that buttons can give. Rich, dark colors work best because they slim the upper bod—layer a brown turtleneck under a matching leather jacket, and add jeans or cream-colored pants on bottom, and a pair of colorful heels to complete the ensemble.

- *Busties:* Open, mandarin-collar jackets are a knockout on Busties. Combine one with the toughness of dark, flared jeans and the softness of a draped-neck or boat-neck tee. Sophisticated leather wedges and a drop necklace are the finishing touches.

- *Booties and Hipsters:* Blazer-inspired styles that fall just below the hip with a slight flare are a match for you. They tuck and tailor your upper bod and soften and flatter your midsection. Create a timeless look with wide-leg slacks, a gauzy top that flows to the hips, and a colorful neck scarf or chunky necklace.

- ***Dainties:*** Get your motor running, girl! Body-hugging biker-inspired leather styles are perfect for your petite frame. Opt for feminine, updated motorcycle jackets that are fitted and not too overloaded with zippers and pockets (or, dare we say it—fringe!). The sleek, higher cut will flatter your frame and accentuate your waist, making the most of your feminine curves. Work the look with slim jeans or capris, a body-hugging hip-length top, and a girly kitten-heel or peep-toe shoe.

————

BELTED AND WRAP: *Cozy* and *sophisticated*—the two words that come to mind when you think about wrapping yourself up in this supremely feminine style. This is the type of jacket you may find yourself wanting to slip into every day, especially when it's designed with light, flexible fabrics (cotton sateen, linen, or stretchy synthetic blends such as polyester, viscose, and Lycra). Belted styles can look easy breezy with cargos and capris or downright devastating with a long black pencil skirt and pumps. Go ahead, wrap it up!

- ***Belly Babes:*** Definitely try this baby on for size. A just-below-hip-length jacket designed with a belt that hits slightly above the waist will add nice shape and definition. Since you can make it as loose or fitted as you want around your midsection, it's a comfy style, too.

- ***Busties:*** Look for fabrics with a little give that will conform to your sexy shape. Jackets without breast pockets are best for you. Stick with simple tops underneath, so your upper body doesn't feel overwhelmed.

- ***Booties and Hipsters:*** Look for up-dated versions of classics, such as feminine safari jackets that cinch at the waist and flare at your hip. Keep your eye out for looser, fluid fabrics (light poplins or silk blends) that flatter rather than cling.

- ***Dainties:*** Stick with shorter, streamlined styles that hit right at the top of the hips and have thin or moderate-size belts about two inches wide. A jacket in an eye-catching punchy color can also add volume to your frame.

COATS: Regardless of your size or shape, the way to go with coats is classic, classic, classic. Get cozy with sophisticated wraps, elegant button-downs, and playful puffers. Have fun spicing up your collection with a few eye-catching pieces here and there—such as an irresistible Missoni-inspired style with colorful zigzag stripes, or an updated plaid—but basic neutrals (black, brown, camel) will be your enduring staples.

- ***Belly Babes:*** Wrap yourself up in A-line empires and belted styles that hit just below the rib cage. Try wearing the collar slightly up for a high dose of sophistication or throw on a vibrant scarf to accentuate your upper body.

- ***Busties:*** Single-breasted belted styles work well for you, since they aren't as confining. Whether you cover up in a springy poplin trench or a cozy cashmere shawl collar, belt it out! Princess coats (with seams that run from your bust down to the hem) are also ideal, as they add shape to your body without binding you in.

- **Booties and Hipsters:** With their flirty flare, trapeze, swing, and A-line styles look lovely on you. The most flattering lengths are just below the knee or at the shin. High-heel boots add just the right finishing touch.

- **Dainties:** You can't miss in double-breasted pea coats or military-inspired styles. Drape yourself in a sumptuous button-down and suddenly your swagger's a whole lot swankier. Or, summon your inner ski bunny with a hip-length puffer.

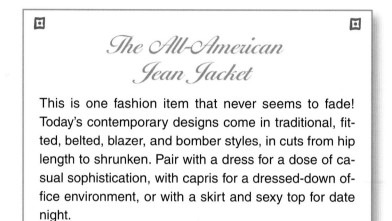

The All-American Jean Jacket

This is one fashion item that never seems to fade! Today's contemporary designs come in traditional, fitted, belted, blazer, and bomber styles, in cuts from hip length to shrunken. Pair with a dress for a dose of casual sophistication, with capris for a dressed-down office environment, or with a skirt and sexy top for date night.

FABULOUS FEMMES

Amy:

With her perfectly petite frame and quick wit, Amy is one feisty Dainty. This Chicago-based writer is a sucker for all things vintage, so her style is a blend of finds from Grandma's closet and her favorite retro boutiques. Just over five feet tall, she's slight enough to fit into children's clothes but feels most at home in her designer duds. Slim and straight, she likes to refer to herself as "Kate Moss-esque minus five inches: with a negligible chest, slim hips, and a straight, long neck."

She is a big sucker for jackets and owns at least seventy-five of them. Amy says that they're the easiest way to pump up a look. She owns tight, cropped leather jackets that she wears with pouf skirts or jeans, and long, roomy, boyish, suit-style jackets that she pairs with skinny jeans and spike heels. Three-quarter-length jackets are another of her favorites to wear with dresses for "a polished look."

Amy also layers longer jackets to avoid overpowering her tiny frame. She balances out a roomier piece with body-skimming tanks or camis and slim-fitting pants. To top it off, she goes right for a pair of killer heels and an armful of mix-and-match gold bangles. Whether she's mixing old and new or fitted and flared, Amy does eclectic in the most excellent way!

Raven:

Aside from having one of the coolest names, Raven is a style goddess! As a luxury lifestyle consultant, she has the exciting job of working closely with a variety of ultraposh brands, and her sense of fashion is impeccable. Often her choices are geared toward showing off her fantastic Curvy bod. "More than once I have been described as 'Rubenesque,' which I take as a major compliment. I love the image of a voluptuous Italian woman, à la Sophia Loren—my idol." Although she looks (and dresses) like perfection to our eyes, she claims to have two outstanding problems: "my Homer Simpson belly and the fact that I have the rib cage of an ox."

Still, she loves to sport pants and jackets—because the effect is utterly feminine and elegant. She favors high-waist, flat-front, wide-leg pants—extra long so that they lengthen her tall body and drape down to the floor. "The high waist somehow camouflages my belly and makes me look taller, even though it shortens my torso a bit."

And since her most flattering features are her décolletage, neck, and broad shoulders, fitted jackets are another must. "Hands down, my favorite item in my wardrobe! I have a *huge* collection of jackets. For me, they are the cure-all. I find that I can throw on a jacket over jeans and a blouse and feel taller and leaner and polished. On a desert island, I would need a fabulous black jacket and nothing else. Black is great, but white is so chic and a favorite of mine."

Many of her jackets don't button but have razor-sharp tailoring that helps them to stay in place. "I need things that are nipped at the waist and then have a peplumlike detail. My frame is straight up and down and thick waisted. So the peplum detail seems to create the illusion that I have a Sophia Loren bod just waiting to bust out!"

Michaela:

Michaela is a fireball! She has infectious energy, perfect glowing skin, a curly mane of I'd-kill-for-it hair, and confidence up the wazoo. As host of one the top morning news and lifestyle television shows in Los Angeles, she is seen by millions every day. But whether she's on camera or off, she always looks stunning. Her clothes don't wear her—she wears the clothes.

She describes herself as "very Curvy—sort of a figure eight . . . not to be confused with a *size* 8." She has a waist and favors clothing styles that play it up to the hilt. She is also a Busty with "a great rack" but chooses things that don't necessarily accentuate it.

Michaela loves a good trouser but has one steadfast rule: "*No* pleating—*please!*" She likes cuffs at the bottom, which lengthen her body, and prefers no pockets on the sides (she will often have them sewn shut to create a leaner line). She tends to stick with darker colors and fabrics that hang well. "I have strong thighs and do not need to add any bulk."

She pairs pants with everything from shirtdresses to tees and long cardigans to belted tunics. Whatever the combo, she is a showstopper, from head to toe!

CHAPTER FOUR

Flirty: Skirts and Sweaters

My, how things have changed! In the 1950s, the skirt and sweater was the *the* look for refined, proper young ladies and a mandate for many school dress codes. In the 1990s, they replaced the power suit worn in the previous decade by business mavens climbing their way to the top. The skirt and sweater have survived many societal standards as well as fashion runways. On their own, each is feminine and timeless, but together they make a couple hotter than Brangelina.

Unlike the dress, the skirt and sweater can be much easier to wear for those of us with tops and bottoms that don't necessarily jive. And for those lucky ladies who are perfectly proportioned, cheers to you . . . the skirt and sweater works like a charm. Bottom line, the skirt and sweater is a bull's-eye, slam dunk, hit-it-out-of-the-ballpark combination that is fabulous for every figure.

Let's deconstruct the skirt, shall we? (We'll get to sweaters later.) It's a pretty simple wardrobe essential; basically, it's a rectangle of fabric wrapped around your waist to cover your lower half. What makes the skirt so alluring is the mystery it holds, the imagination it elicits, and the many personalities it assumes. It's romantic yet professional. It's playful but also serious. You can bum on the beach in a skirt, or meet the president in one. It is a chameleon that can suit any mood and master any occasion.

When it comes to skirts, hem lengths rise and fall faster than pop stars. One year, the must-have is a micromini, and the next year, it's a long, gypsy skirt. Fret not. Keep the basics of your skirt wardrobe classic, then mix in some seasonal trends. Whether long or short, there's no skirting the issue— this is one garment that matches your mood and brings out your inner siren.

Bounce in Your Flounce

HALL OF FAME

A skirt is like a great glass of wine. When it's in the glass, you may notice the color and the texture, but inhale its aroma, take a sip, swirl it around your mouth and taste the complexities hidden within. The same thing happens when you match a simple skirt with a zesty top or sweater. Despite its simplicity, the skirt weaves together proportions, textures, details, and colors, making it the Cabernet Sauvignon of your wardrobe. If choosing a skirt is as foreign to you as identifying wines, no worries. We're here to help. It doesn't have to be so complicated. Just think **smooth, jersey knit, pull-on, fluid, knee-length, and A-line**.

- *Smooth.* Pockets, pleats, gathering, and buttons can sometimes draw unwanted attention. By keeping it smooth, you eliminate unwanted heft and allow the fabric to do all the work. A fabric that lays smooth is most flattering to the curves of your body.

- *Jersey knit.* We love this fabric. Not only is it supersoft and comfy, but it keeps you looking slim and trim. Find one that is matte in a mid to light weight that covers your bumps and calls out your curves. If it's too thick, it takes on a mind of its own; but if it's too thin, it will show every dimple.

- **Pull-on.** A zipper can call attention to your midsection, rump, or hips, depending on its placement. We prefer a pull-on skirt with a wider and thicker waistband, to prevent the bunching and puffing that can occur with a thin, elastic waist. Generally, a pull-on skirt has a little Lycra in it or other stretchy material that helps the skirt slide and glide over your curves.

- **Fluid.** A skirt that drapes elegantly and gracefully over your hips, bum, and tum allows the fabric to move with your body. A fluid fabric creates motion and emphasizes your feminine form, whereas a stiff fabric can hang listlessly and make you look boxy.

- **Knee-length.** Not too conservative and steering clear from risqué, a skirt that lands at or just below the knee is appropriate for a woman of any age. It's a classic length that takes the guesswork out of how much leg to show.

- **A-line.** Named for its similarity in shape to the letter *A*, the A-line skirt slims your waist and flows over hips and thighs. It widens gradually from top to bottom and is designed to flatter almost every figure. We don't just give the A-line skirt an A; we give it an A+.

FIT TO FLAUNT

Prepare to get leggy with it. The skirt is all about showing off those gams. But let's not forget about the rear view. The right blend of fit and fabric can flaunt for days.

- Hem lengths aren't the only thing that rise and fall with current trends—waistlines do, too. For this reason, make sure to try on your skirts with different tops and sweaters, to see where they fall. You may think you finally found the perfect skirt for that top that's been waiting for the perfect mate in the back of your closet, only to be disappointed when the skirt sits an inch too short and shows off your midriff. A skirt may also have detailing, such as ties or piping, that gets lost under or sticks through your tops.

- We've seen them under slacks, but even worse (and often more obvious) is a visible panty line (so lovingly nicknamed, VPL) under your skirt. Try on skirts with the right panties—we prefer thongs—or hose with a built-in panty, to avoid clinging and bunching. You could always go the au natural route of the true Scotsman and his kilt (wink, wink), but to avoid any accidental flashes, we suggest sticking with the thong.

- How does the skirt fit your waist? If it's too loose, it can become boxy and shapeless. If it's too tight, it can accentuate areas by creating bulges and creases. You want a comfortable fit around your waist that allows breathing space but keeps the skirt in place.

- Legs always look better in heels. They pump up your calves as if you've been climbing the stairs all day. To give your ego a boost, try your skirts on with shoes—from ballet flats to stilettos, you'll see what looks saintly and what looks sinful. Depending on the shoe you choose, you can create varying levels of height.

- Imagine yourself wearing this skirt with different tops, shoes, and accessories. Now picture yourself at different events. Is the skirt versatile? The best choice is one you can wear for any occasion. If you're on the run from home to work to a night on the town (perhaps all in a single day!), your clothes need to accommodate your schedule. Make sure the skirt can keep up when, to show off your silky cami top, you shed the cardigan you wore to work. Then slip on strappy heels and you're ready for the night.

SKIRTS 101

WRAP: As much as we all love our jeans, a wrap skirt is a flirty substitute when we want to show a little skin. Paired with a T-shirt and flip-flops on a casual Sunday or with a sparkling halter top and strappy sandals on a first date, the wrap skirt is comfortable and easy to wear by any body shape for any occasion. From turtleneck to tank, make sure the top you choose to wear with your wrap skirt lies flat and smooth so that it doesn't add extra bulk or end up in a wrestling match with the tie of the skirt.

- ***Booties and Hipsters:*** Because it sits close to the waist, the wrap skirt is a great choice for you. It flows over your hips, backside, and thighs while accentuating your trim waist and creating a more hourglass shape. Choose deep, solid colors or a vertical print and match it with a top that shows a little skin. An open neckline or bare shoulders can help finish off the balancing act.

- ***Belly Babes:*** The flexibility afforded by the adjustable waist on the wrap skirt makes this one belly-licious. You are in the driver's seat with this skirt controlling the fit of the waist. Loosen it a bit and you'll happily steer clear of "muffin-top" syndrome. And because it drapes softly over the hips, it will draw the attention away from your midsection.

- ***Leggies:*** One thing that makes the wrap skirt unique is its layering effect. Many styles wrap around your body and land in layers. This can really work to your advantage, Leggies, by breaking up the length of your lower half. Pair it with a top that plays up your torso and arms . . . something with a V-neck or long, fitted sleeves.

- ***Dainties:*** For your sweet stature, the wrap skirt stands tall on our list. They tend to sit at your true waist, so find one that lands below the knee or midcalf for extra length. The layering of this skirt should sit close to your body rather than adding fullness. Throw on tall boots or heavenly heels, and the sky's the limit for you.

A-LINE: Wear it high around your waist, or slung low above your hips. Either way, you'll make the grade with the A-line skirt. It's more tapered at the top and widens at the bottom, providing extra room in the hip, waist, and tummy. You want a perfect fit around your waist, and this skirt should graze over your hips and backside. A skirt that gradually extends to a slight flair at the bottom is the most flattering.

- ***Booties and Hipsters:*** This is a great skirt for you! Look for one that is a little more tailored. If it widens too much, too fast, it can look sloppy, so keep it crisp and clean. To balance its fuller hemline, show off your upper body with a square or cowl neckline.

- ***Belly Babes:*** Because the A-line skirt widens from top to bottom, it draws the eye down with it, so play up those sexy stems. Since everyone will be busy admiring your legs, make sure they are decorated with a great pair of shoes or boots. This skirt also narrows at the waist, creating a tapered look where you like it most.

- ***Leggies:*** How lovely is an A-line skirt with a pair of ballet slippers or mules? We love it, and we love it on you because it shows off your great length. Wear it low on your waist and match it with a long top or sweater for a sleek look. Add a low-slung belt and boots, and you are TDF—to die for!

- ***Dainties:*** An A-line skirt not only emphasizes your waist but it also elongates your shape. It's great whether you are a short-waisted or long-waisted Dainty: if you're short-waisted, opt for a narrower waistband; whereas if you're long-waisted, you'll knock 'em out with a thicker waistband. Either way, by defining your waist, you'll successfully balance your top and bottom halves and create height.

PENCIL: Some fashionistas may pontificate about pencil skirts' being appropriate only for tall women (hello . . . Leggies). We aren't fans of discriminating that way and believe that the pencil skirt is, in fact, a great skirt for any body type. Because the pencil skirt has a fitted waist, a tailored fit through the hips, and a tapered hemline, it shows off curves if you've got them and creates them if you don't. While it should hug your body, you want to be able to move, sit, and breathe comfortably. However, if you feel like a stuffed sausage after a few nibbles or a light lunch, it's time for something with a little more give.

- ***Booties and Hipsters:*** This skirt puts the beauty in booty! Your bubbly backside will be the star in a pencil skirt—its natural curved shape was made for you Hipsters. It worked for Marilyn Monroe and it will work for you. A dark skirt with a brightly colored top or sweater keeps you looking slim and trim. A little slit in the back will make it easier to get around and, for a little extra flair, you can deviate from the traditional pencil skirt and find one with a fishtail shape.

- ***Belly Babes:*** The simplicity and smoothness of the pencil skirt is what makes it great for you, Belly Babes. With a little stretch at the waist and without pockets, belt loops, pleats, gathering, and buttons, the pencil skirt keeps the focus off of the midsection and instead aims it at the legs, hips, and bottom. Woo-hoo! Slip into a soft, banded-bottom sweater, and you're ready for the runway.

- ***Leggies:*** This skirt has your name all over it. If you're a gal who embraces her lengthy legs, find a pencil skirt that hits just below the knee, one that you can wear high on your waist. Tuck in a silky blouse for a sophisticated look. You can also break up the length by wearing the skirt lower on your waist with a longer, form-fitting sweater. A wide belt finishes off either combination.

- ***Dainties:*** The long lines of the pencil skirt can really work to your advantage. Stay afloat with a skirt that makes its mark right at your knee; any lower, and you'll end up drowning in a sea of fabric. Bows, ribbons, and such details as buttons can overpower your smaller stature, so keep it clean and smooth. To make your legs look longer and give you the appearance of added height, opt for a darker-colored skirt. Round it out with a pair of close-toe heels for length and fluidity.

———

STRAIGHT: In its basic design, the straight skirt may not seem so exciting. It hangs straight from the hips down and is usually tapered at the waist. However, it is a staple that every woman should have in her closet. You can dress it up or dress it down, and because of its simplicity the straight skirt will never go out of style. Variations of the straight skirt give it a little extra flare, as well. A trouser skirt is a straight skirt meant to resemble a pair of men's trousers, complete with pockets, belt loops, and fly front. For a little more sass, show off your gams with a straight miniskirt. Because of its simplicity, the straight skirt is a delight in virtually any fabric, including cotton, satin, knit, denim, and leather.

- ***Booties and Hipsters:*** For you ladies, the fabric is important when it comes to a straight skirt. A fabric that drapes well with a comfortable fit will flow nicely over your hips and booty without clinging. Single layer, rather than lined, skirts don't bunch as much and keep you looking smooth. If pockets are your pleasure, go for side pockets (without a lining) that are cut at an angle. This extra angled line will create a narrowing effect on your hips. Pair with a cowl- or square-neck sweater to broaden your shoulders and balance your bod.

- ***Belly Babes:*** A straight skirt with front and side seams shift the focus downwards, as does a slit—we like a sexy little slit in either the front or back, depending on the style of the skirt. A dark, soft, lightweight denim skirt with some stretch and that sits no lower than the bottom of your knee is supersexy when paired with tall boots.

- ***Leggies:*** Like the pencil skirt, the straight skirt is another winner for you Leggies. A straight skirt that hits you right at or just below the knee is most flattering. You will find that it keeps you looking long and tall without added height. Although some fashion hit-or-miss lists may suggest that ladies with the long legs avoid miniskirts, we say go for it. A low-waist mini that hits midthigh matched with a pair of boots that comes to your knee is a showstopper. Add a long and lean sweater to create harmony between your torso and your long legs. Very hot!

- ***Dainties:*** From the bottom of the thigh to the knee, a straight skirt is great for adding length. Find one with big, bold, vertical patterns such as swirls, asymmetric designs, or vertical lines for some zip. Add a solid-colored wrap top or sweater or a V-neck to perfectly balance from top to bottom. An open-toe wedge or sandal is your best bet with this skirt.

––––––––

GATHERED: When we think of gathered skirts, the image of women toting tall glasses of lager and draped in layers of fabric can't help but come to mind. The *dirndl,* as it's called, may be a traditional gathered skirt (and girlfriend to the lederhosen), but it's not quite what we picture as the epitome of high fashion. Then again, stranger things have made appearances on the catwalks of New York and Paris. For our definition of a gathered skirt, think loose folds, ruching, pleats, and tiers.

- ***Booties and Hipsters:*** Yes, you can wear gathered skirts. When they're chosen well your hip hugging curves and backside bundle are a mighty force. Look for full, vertical pleats that start midthigh. Keep it more fitted through the hips and bottom, with a bit of fullness lower on the skirt. Try a style with soft gathers paired with a V-neck top or sweater, tall boots, and a wide belt, and your dance card will be full.

- **Belly Babes:** Soft folds and low pleats will widen your hips and thin your waist. With this skirt, it's all about creating harmony, so be mindful of the cut. Look for front ruching—it adds texture to your tummy area, making it lean and lovely.

- **Leggies:** Since you already have the height with those lusciously long legs, you can go horizontal with a divided or tiered skirt. You can also go longer with this style; midcalf works to your advantage with a tiered skirt. Gypsy skirts with bead or jewel embellishments, matched with a pair of leather sandals, is pure bohemian chic. Add a hemline ruffle and your style is sweet and demure.

- **Dainties:** Exploit the vertical lines of a pleated or gathered skirt, to create height. This can be a really fun and flirty look for you. Cinch it in with a wide belt: the combination of the gentle fullness of the skirt with the smooth and long waist created by the belt will transform your look entirely. Add heels, and you can give any NBA great a run for his money . . . at least when it comes to fashion.

What a Waist

Long waisted means the distance between your shoulders and waist is longer than average, or that you have a longer torso. *Short waisted* means the distance between your shoulders and waist is shorter than average, or that you have a shorter torso. For long-waisted lovelies, high-waisted skirts with vertical lines and a tucked-in top can add length to your legs. Short-waisted sassies can lengthen their torso by wearing skirts lower on the hips, with longer tops.

Sassy in Sweaters

HALL OF FAME

Sexy, sassy, scintillating, and even sweet, the sweater has proven itself to be more than functional. When you slip one on, it should hug your curves and show off your assets, giving you a sense of what it means to be a daring diva who's ready to face the world. It should keep you warm without sending you into hot flashes; it should be soft on your skin; and it should allow you range of movement without rising, binding, or bunching. With so many choices between pullovers and cardigans, and among weaves and fabrics, choosing a sweater can wind a girl up tighter than a ball of yarn. Relax, take a deep breath, and stay fabulously feminine with **V-neck, soft, smooth, snug, long-sleeve, and hip-length.**

- *V-neck.* The V-neck sweater is flattering on almost every body type. The openness created by the V balances out lower body drama while lengthening upper-body drama. It defines a girl's shape and form in all the right places.

- *Soft.* With something so close to your skin, make sure it's soft and comfortable. The perfect sweater is one that you could wear every day. A good litmus test is to ask yourself: If these were sheets, would I sleep in them?

- *Smooth.* Cashmere, Moreno wool, pima cotton, and silk blends not only feel good, they lay well on your body. These fabrics tend to be midweight, which provide structure without overpowering.

- *Snug.* Instead of a boxy- or bulky-looking sweater, we prefer knits that are "form flattering," meaning they are fitted—even in shoulders and arms—but not tight (jelly rolls may be tasty, but they seem to lose their delectability once they've found their way to the midriff). It should be snug enough to define your waist and show off your other curves, while still allowing you ease of movement.

- *Long-sleeve.* Sure, little cap-sleeve sweaters are cute (and often frilly), and 3/4-length sleeves are always a winner, but our all-time favorite is a long-sleeve sweater. It goes with pretty much everything from skirts to slacks to jeans.

- *Hip-length.* Sweater length can vary from under the breast (bolero) to the knee. We say, aim for something smack in the middle—the hips. A sweater that falls to the hips creates length in the torso and adds fluidity to a full-length sleeve.

FIT TO FLAUNT

From body-skimming to long and cozy, what you want is finding an elegant, all-over fit that doesn't bulk you up. Whether you're decked out in cotton, silk, or cashmere, a trusty sweater oozes femininity.

- Because different woven and knit fabrics vary in how they cling to the body, make sure to try on your sweaters with different bras. A clean, unbroken line is what you're after, so make sure that the sweater doesn't bunch around the bra. Generally seamless, smooth-cup bras are a good match for a sweater. Also because your front is featured in a sweater, keep "the girls" high and proud in a well-fitting, supportive bra.

- Is the knit on your sweater so large that it looks like a chain-link fence? Okay, that might be an exaggeration, but some sweaters do have a wider knit and some cottons can be very sheer, leaving you a little more exposed than you might like. The solution is simple: a camisole or other appropriate undergarment can cover you in just the right spots.

- Make sure the material feels good against your skin. Because sweaters are often made from natural animal fibers such as wool and angora, they may itch or cause a reaction. It's not so pretty to walk around scratching and itching or with big red blotches on your skin. If this is a problem, go with silks and cottons, which tend to be more gentle. Another consequence of natural fibers: shedding. Soft, fuzzy fabrics such as angora or alpaca can leave more hair behind than a Persian cat. Be sure to test sweaters for this or you may end up with fur that sticks like Velcro.

- Sweaters keep us warm, but they should also be breathable. Air passing in and out of the sweater will keep you temperate, and the most breathable fabrics are natural ones. Often synthetics (and unfortunately some wools) can absorb body odors and, no matter how many times the sweater is dry-cleaned or washed, the odor just won't seem to go away.

- Don't forget to check the cleaning instructions on your sweaters. Are they dry-clean only or hand wash? If so, you could rack up some hefty cleaning bills or wear the sweater once and let it sit in the bottom of your hamper waiting to be hand washed. It's important to note that wools often shrink when improperly washed, and may need to dry flat, so pay extra attention to the care instructions on your wool sweaters.

SWEATERS 101

V-NECK: One of the best things about the V-neck is that it calls attention to the face. No matter what issues you've got goin' on below the neck, when you're wearing a V-neck they all seem to disappear. So, slip on that V-neck, slab on some lip gloss, and you'll be ready for your close-up.

- *Busties:* This is, hands down, one of the best necklines for you. It may seem counterintuitive to show off your cleavage, but the V actually elongates your body and creates openness in your chest giving you a slimmer look. When you cover up a big bust, it tends to look bigger, so go ahead and let the sunshine in. Minimize accessories to a pair of eye-catching earrings.

- *Tatas:* Although this cut may minimize the bustier gals, it will have an opposite effect on you, Tatas. By showing off your cleavage, the V-neck creates the illusion of a larger chest when needed. Embellishments along the neckline enhance the effect. You might also try layering a deep V (you can go low with it because of your smaller chest) over a tank or cami top that peeks out from underneath.

- *Belly Babes:* Because the V-neck draws attention up toward your face, there's no need to worry about a little too much tummy. Keep the focus high with some great jewelry—a chunky necklace will do just the trick. The other benefit of a V-neck sweater is that it slenderizes an otherwise round or square midsection.

- *Broads:* Because it creates more of a vertical movement than a horizontal one, the V-neck sweater helps slenderize broad shoulders. The openness and angles of the neckline add to the effect. If you have a smaller bust, try a deep-V sweater layered over a cami top, for an even more dramatic lengthening effect.

ROUND-NECK: Crew, scoop, and boatnecks all fall under the realm of a sweater with a rounded neck. Basically any sweater with a rounded neckline will work for us. Whether it's closer to the neck or closer to the cleavage is icing on the delicious chocolate cake.

- *Busties:* Rather than a higher-cut rounded neckline such as a crew neck, a scoop or boatneck is more up your alley. By showing a little skin, you elongate your neck and prevent your bust from looking like an extension of your chin. Mega-boobs, be gone! Also, the neckline on these sweaters frames your face. Play it up with a semi-chunky necklace that sits close to your collarbone.

- *Tatas:* Do it up with details. Often crew-neck tops have a ribbed or banded neckline. This type of detail can really give you a leg (or boob!) up by helping to fill you out. Wider necklines such as boatnecks create a more defined shape to your upper body, as well.

- *Belly Babes:* The openness of these necklines draws attention away from your tummy. Whether you are a little full in the waist or are sporting a pooch, a sweater with a rounded neck and a banded bottom that sits low on your hips will create a balanced look from the top to the bottom of your torso. Any yummy stuffing in the middle will just seem to fade away.

Let's Neck

When it comes to necklines, there's more to consider than your body shape. Also think about what you've got going on from the neck up. The shape of your face can play a big role in what necklines work for you. A wider face benefits from lower or deeper necklines, such as scoop and V-necks that create a vertical line; whereas a longer, narrower face looks great with wider necklines such as boat and crew necks.

- ***Broads:*** Scoop and crew necks keep the neckline opening closer to the neck, which can help to minimize shoulders, by creating a line of vision closer to the center of the chest; A deeper scoop neck accentuates the effect by adding a vertical element. Toss on a long, dangling necklace and you're ready to roll.

———

WRAP: Every present is fun to unwrap! The layering of fabric and the diagonal lines created by a wrap sweater flatter many figures. Because necklines vary from high to deep, you might need to add an extra layer, such as a tank top or camisole, underneath the sweater.

- ***Busties:*** Wrap sweaters are a great choice for Busties because they give you the flexibility to adjust the sweater for the size of your chest. They also often drape lower across the chest, either in a scoop or a V-neck, both of which are flattering for your curves. Also, the tie on this sweater helps to accentuate your waist and create space under your breasts. Just make sure that the sweater falls to your hips, to take advantage of this unique style.

- ***Tatas:*** Layers and details. Need we say more? A wrap sweater that closes right around the top of the cleavage worn over a tank, cami, or other undergarment will do the trick. The diagonal lines created by the sweater's layers will fall around your chest accentuating the bustline. Added detailing such as picot or ribbed trim add further emphasis, turning your tatas into *tatas*!

- ***Belly Babes:*** We've said it before and we'll say it again, we love anything that wraps on Belly Babes. The layers help cover your belly without adding bulk and the tapering of the waist from the tie highlights your hips. A more open wrap sweater with a loosely collared neckline worn over a cotton cami will bring all eyes upward.

- ***Broads:*** The asymmetrical lines created by the wrap sweater draw the eye away from your shoulders. This sweater tends to create vertical and diagonal movement across an otherwise square frame. In a wrap sweater, Broads appear to have a smaller waist, shapely hips, and an overall proportioned figure.

TURTLENECK: Folded, rolled, scrunched, straight, half, and mock—there are many variations on the turtleneck, with one similar goal: to create a long, lean neck. All hail to the turtleneck for keeping the turkey necks at bay so the foxy femmes can play.

- *Busties:* Straight and half-neck turtlenecks suit you best, Busties. Folded or rolled necks tend to rob you of cleavage and create a solid mass that takes the form of one big breast. To restore order, make sure the sweater is fitted to call out your curves, and that its bottom sits low by your hips. Simple vertical knit detailing or ribbing will also help achieve a leaner look.

- *Tatas:* Because the turtleneck is long and can often flatten your chest, add accessories to bring the "ta-da" into Tatas. Long necklaces (we're talking belly button long) with chunky details, hoops, or layers of chains can fast-track a turtleneck to a winning finish.

- *Belly Babes:* Fabrics with some texture or a little give are going to be your best bet, when it comes to turtlenecks. Some cottons and wools are more forgiving if they fit a little looser or have stretch, but you don't want it to feel bulky. A simple vertical knit or stitch will slim down your middle. A turtleneck that is a little tapered at the waist can also help.

Rule the Empire

The empire style works for pretty much everyone because it has a fitted chest with a looser-fitting, flowing midsection. It covers tummies and hips, and helps to narrow bottoms. It creates curves where they don't exist and can add or subtract height, depending on the length of the sweater. For mommies-to-be the empire sweater is a great garment that you can continue to wear even after baby arrives.

- **Broads:** Turtlenecks have a tendency to square off the shoulders. To counter this, play up your waist and hips with a turtleneck that is fitted through the waist and gently flares at the hips. Another option is a longer turtleneck with a wide belt slung low on the hips. Add an A-line skirt in denim or suede with tall boots that hit your knees. The flare of the skirt, along with the heavier fabric and the weight of the boots, will really give your bottom half some oomph!

––––––

COWL NECK: It's a bit ironic that a sweater that elicits so much sex appeal had its foundation in religion—cowls were the hooded garments originally worn by monks! Thankfully, they transitioned well into high fashion. We love cowl necks because they add shape and create balance for almost every figure. Amen!

- **Busties:** A lightweight, low-cut cowl neck is supersexy on you. Make sure the fabric is thinner or lightweight; a bulky cowl neck will add to the weightiness of your breasts. This type of sweater already has a lot going on, so keep the rest of it simple—jeans with heels, or an A-line skirt with tall boots. Between the fabric and your breasts, a necklace will just get lost, so stick with long dangling earrings for a fun evening look.

- **Tatas:** What better way to bulk up your boobs than with a cowl neck. Go for the gusto with this one. A large, bulky collar or heavy detailing will play up your upper body and add volume to your chest. Keep it simple and clean on the bottom with this sweater. A pencil or straight skirt will make the fluffiness of the cowl neck look even more fabulous.

- **Belly Babes:** By the sweater's creating extra bulk on the upper part of your torso, your tummy will seem to fade away into oblivion. So, stock up on cowl necks—they look great on you. One with a banded waist will help blouse the body of the sweater. On the other hand, a longer sweater that hits you low on the hips, with an open or unstructured bottom, is superfine with straight-leg jeans.

- **Broads:** How low can you go? Loosely draping fabrics (silk blends, cottons, and some wools) that form a low-hanging cowl will create long, vertical lines on you and help soften your shoulders. The long, circular, almost U shape of the cowl will move eyes up and down your body rather than across it. Don't worry about going too low; just throw on a little cami under the sweater to cover up.

CARDIGAN: Nothing is as classic as a cardigan sweater. Hang one over your shoulders, toss one over your tops, or layer them with camis. You really can't go wrong with the cardigan. Although button-ups are the more traditional cardigans, we might also consider zip fronts, ties, and wrap styles as cardigans, too. As long as it opens down the front, it's a cardigan to us.

- **Busties:** If you don't want your boobs to look like they end at your waist, think long. Your cardigans should hit you at your hips. A V- or sweetheart neckline is also a good style for you when it comes to cardigans. Keep in mind that you have all the control with this sweater: you can show off a little cleavage by unbuttoning a button or two or bringing the zipper down a bit. Showing a little skin will brighten your face and lengthen your torso.

- **Tatas:** A crisp, collared shirt under your cardigan is going to add shape and structure to your upper bod. You might also go a little preppy and tie the cardigan around your shoulders so that it drapes over your chest. If you have a smaller frame, you might consider tucking in your top under your sweater, to create a blousy look. This will also define your waist, which will help to simulate additional curves. Opt for necklines with a little more shape, such as V-, sweetheart, or scoop necks. Extra detailing around the neck such as simple beading or stitch work, will enhance your chest.

- **Belly Babes:** Being able to layer the cardigan is what works best for you. By "layer" we're not suggesting a sweater set throwback to the 1950s. Instead, think of tops you can wear peeking out from inside your cardigans: tanks, camis, blouses, V-necks, and yes, other sweaters. Whatever you choose, keep it long and untucked. Low-sitting pockets are also a plus, not only because of the extra fabric, but because of the lines they create.

- **Broads:** Wear your cardigans open. The vertical lines created by wearing this sweater open will really balance out your shoulders. If you do want to close shop, opt for a cardigan with extra detailing. A hood or some lower-placed pockets will maintain the vertical element, as will eye-catching buttons.

FABULOUS FEMMES

Raven:

When Busty and Hipster Raven slips on a skirt—which is often—she looks like something straight out of the golden age of Hollywood—Rita Hayworth, Grace Kelly, and her idol, Sophia Loren, all rolled into one. "Skirts are my favorite things to wear. I love all shapes. I do really well in the sexy secretary look—a fitted high-waist pencil with a flare."

She looks for styles with waistbands that "contain and flatten my belly" and then flare out from there. Raven loves all fabrics, colors, and patterns, but the constant in her choices is that they all have a feminine and timeless feel.

Raven often pairs pencil skirts with tailored button-downs that have a bit of detail, or ultrathin knits or cashmere sweaters. They don't add bulk and "you can see my shape."

Deena:

Deena goes against the grain and often shows up at the office in skirt and sweater combos. No pantsuits for this girl! "I love a good-fitting pencil skirt. I have a few in black, a few in different denims, and a couple in stripes and plaids." Her current favorite is a classic, cream-colored silk that falls above the knee. She loves the versatility of pencil skirts—"They look great belted or with shirts tucked in or out, sweaters, jackets, and more"—along with the way they play up her feminine figure.

One of Deena's most flattering combos is a straight skirt and cardigan. "I'm probably more partial to sweaters that have a little bit of a funky detail or pattern or something to make them stand out." Clever girl!

Barb:

Although Barb claims to "prefer dresses to skirts," you'd never know it by seeing how she rocks it in one of these! She takes her signature mix of dark neutrals and applies it to skirts by mixing sultry fabrics, layering unexpected touches such as a leather bomber jacket, or funking it up with knee-high boots.

Barb opts for styles that accentuate her waist, whether it's a slinky, silky pencil skirt with a pleated bottom, or a flirty, flared skirt paired with a crisp white button-down. She always pairs her skirts with eye-catching tops to keep them from looking too formal or overly tailored. Sexy is what it's all about!

Yasmine:

Stretchy cotton skirts are a weekly regular in Yasmine's work wardrobe. They offer a put-together look that is supercomfy and flowing. Yasmine loves to layer long tanks underneath tees and sweaters, for a modern look that flaunts and flatters her curves without being too revealing. When it's cool out, she'll often add a pair of cut-off tights. Of course, the cherry on top is a pair of heels.

CHAPTER FIVE

Dressy: Casual and Cocktail Dresses

Cleopatra ruled in them. Marie Antoinette was famous for them. Virginia Woolf wrote in them. Audrey Hepburn was flawless in them. Diana Ross crooned in them. And, Mother Teresa was saintly in them.

Women have changed the world while wearing dresses, and like the great women who have worn them, the allure of the dress withstands the test of time. When it comes to fashion, the dress is the pinnacle of femininity. There is no equivalent in a man's wardrobe (except maybe a Roman toga, and how many men do you know with one of those in their closet?), making it purely feminine. Whether it's big and fluffy or sleek and simple, nothing says "woman" like a dress. Perfect for any occasion from a stroll down the beach to a black-tie gala, the dress always rules.

Perhaps the dress has had such success over the years because of its simplicity. Unlike skirts, pants, blouses and sweaters that need to be mixed and matched, the dress is one-stop shopping. Sure, it may have lots of embellishments, but the basic building block is a single article of clothing. It's pretty much a no-brainer, which makes the dress tops (no pun intended) in our book.

Casual dresses are called for any time of year. In the summer, throw on a sundress with some flip-flops or wedge sandals, and you are prepped for a backyard barbecue. In the winter, tights and tall boots take a wool dress to new levels while you scour the stores for holiday gifts.

When the occasion calls for something with a little more "ta-da," a cocktail dress can be dressed up for a formal affair or dressed down for a fun night of dancing. Strappy heels, a little bling, and a whole lotta fun lovin' attitude will get you far in your favorite cocktail dress.

Gals, have fun with your dresses. Bauble them up, play with boots, sandals, and heels, and experiment with such accessories as bags, wraps, and stockings. And most important, have fun!

Dress It Up

HALL OF FAME

Hem lengths may rise and fall, but one thing that's certain is that the dress is always a constant. From daring to demure, there is a dress for you to get dolled up in. To simplify your life, find one or two that you can spruce up or chill in, and your fashion quandaries will be put to rest. When you have that one go-to dress, you can feel fresh, sexy, and feminine in a snap.

The casual dress that makes our Hall of Fame is the empire-waist dress. Because it has so many incarnations from spaghetti straps to long sleeves, it is a style that transcends the seasons. In the summer, a gauzy, strappy empire-waist dress with sandals, flats, or wedge heels is foolproof for those warm, sunny days. When the weather turns cold, an empire-waist dress with long sleeves can easily be paired with a sexy slingback or tights and boots.

With so many options for cocktail dresses, choosing one favorite can be a brainteaser. Our Hall of Fame choice for cocktail dresses is the wrap dress.

A wrap dress in a dark color suits virtually every figure and, like the empire dress, comes in different styles, such as halters or long sleeves. Although every woman should have a little black dress in her closet, our cocktail Hall-of-Famer thinks beyond the LBD. There are so many lush, rich colors—such as emerald green, burgundy, navy, and chocolate brown—that you can find something deep and dark that makes your skin tone pop.

Both of these styles, the empire-waist dress and the wrap dress, have some similarities that make them our Hall of Fame winners. When looking for the perfect casual or cocktail dress think: **fitted, shaped, flowing, versatile, and knee-length**.

- **Fitted.** A dress with a comfortable fit will play up your natural curves. Something that conforms to your figure without clinging or being too blousy will highlight your bust, whittle your waist, and flatter your hips.

- **Shaped.** The top of the dress should have shape to it, which is why empire-waist and wrap dresses are favorites. The scoop neck on the empire waist and the V on the wrap opens your chest and creates a long and slim look.

- **Flowing.** The bottom of the dress should drape down your body. We're not talking "play hide-and-seek behind the curtains" type of draping, rather fabric that is elegantly loose and flowing for a flawless fit.

- **Versatile.** A versatile dress that can transform from day to night will simplify your life tenfold, particularly on those busy days. Add a jacket, take away a sweater, swap necklaces and earrings, or slip on a different pair of shoes, and you have multiple looks with one dress.

- **Knee-length.** As we said before, hem lengths rise and fall, but you are always on the right track with a classic knee-length dress. A knee-length hemline works day or night for both casual and cocktail dresses. It entices with just enough leg and a little mystery.

FIT TO FLAUNT

Who doesn't love to try on a dress! No matter what kind of day we're having they just seem to be the finest of pick-me-ups. And, they're fun, flirty and oh so feminine.

- Try on the dress with your shoes. Adding a pair of heels, flats, or boots can alter the way the dress looks on your body, and more importantly, the way your legs look. You want the lines of your legs from the hem to your shoe to be seamless. Think of your shoes as the period at the end of an exclamation point!

- Check the fit in your shoulders and cleavage. Do the shoulder straps slip down? If so, they may need an adjustment by the tailor. Does the neckline bare a little too much bust or reveal your bra? See if you can wear a bralette or cami underneath a super-low-cut neckline.

- Move around in it. By this, we mean twist, walk, reach, and sashay in the dress. You are checking to see if the fabric clings, bunches, pulls, or slips. When you sit and cross your legs, does the hemline rise up too high? Avoid a tabloid-worthy disaster by noticing how the fit changes as you move your body.

- Most dressing room light shines from above, but a dress may reveal much more when the light is behind you. Check the dress in different lights to find out if it's see-through. *You* want to be in the spotlight, not your thong.

- Think about special undergarments that the dress needs. Slips and special bras such as halters, strapless, or low-back styles can make a big difference in the way a dress looks. A little lift and support can go a long way.

- Read care labels before purchasing. Unless you want your dry cleaner as your new best friend, choose dresses that you can clean and care for on your own. Dry-clean-only garments are fine for special occasions, but they can be costly to clean when worn regularly. The good news is that it's often easy to wear a dress a couple of times before having to clean it (that is, if you avoided any spills or lots of perspiring).

DRESSES 101

SHIFT DRESS: Jackie O and Audrey Hepburn were two fabulous women who wore the shift well. Making its debut in 1957, the shift dress and its loose-fitting shape was warmly welcomed by women who were tired of the confining dresses that preceded it; most dresses at the time cinched at the waist. The shift hangs straight from the shoulders, usually with minimal tailoring such as breast darts, side panels, or an A-line that skims the body. The shift became a quick classic because of its versatility and its ability to keep silhouettes looking slender. It's tailored for a day at work, but sexy for a night out.

- ***Booties and Hipsters:*** Yes, you too can work the shift dress. Look for one with an interesting neckline and sleeves, to draw the eye upward. Dark colors and large patterns on a medium to heavy fabric that skims over your bottom half will keep everything smooth.

- ***Dainties:*** This is your dress! A shift in a solid color with its straight, narrow cut adds oodles of length to your petite rame. Because the shift generally sits just above the knee, you can show off your legs while making them look longer.

- **Busties:** A shift with a broad, low-cut neckline breaks up your upper half and creates distance between your chin and your bust. Bust darts will tailor the top and create a curvy rather than a straight silhouette.

- **Belly Babes:** Go retro! Ride the throwback of the shift all the way, and go for big, fun patterns. Circles, swirls, waves, boxes, and paisleys in large, vertical patterns will keep that tummy looking trim. Because this dress hangs straight from the shoulders, it's perfect to flatter that babe-alicious belly.

––––––––

HALTER DRESS: Whether you're throwin' it on after a day at the beach or glammin' it up for a hot date, the halter dress is a great choice. A halter top fastens behind the neck, leaving the arms, back, and shoulders bare. Very often the bodice extends to tie at the nape, but variations on the dress include spaghetti straps, a twist at the collar bone, or wide straps. Usually the dress tapers below the bust and has a fuller skirt. Because of the halter's active neckline, keep the necklace in the jewelry box and dazzle it up with a great pair of earrings (dangly, sparkly ones at night give the stars in the sky a run for their money).

- **Booties and Hipsters:** The halter dress works for you on so many levels. The lines created by the top of the dress naturally add width to the shoulders and balance your frame, while the flowing skirt keeps your lower half under wraps. Look for one with wider straps or ties.

- **Dainties:** Because the straps on this dress extend up the chest and behind the neck, it creates long lines for you. For both slim and curvy Dainties, a halter that is cinched at the bust works in your favor.

- **Busties:** Every Busty should have at least one halter dress in her closet. It worked for Marilyn Monroe, and it can work for you! Find one with broader straps that extend from the bodice—you will get a little extra lift and support and the V-neckline will show off your cleavage. A supportive halter bra will help prevent the straps from cutting into the back of your neck.

- **Belly Babes:** With a structured bust, cinching below the bustline, and a fuller skirt, the halter dress is beautiful on Belly Babes. Dark fabrics with at least a medium weight, along with the nice flow, will help keep you looking slim and trim. A V-neckline, with ties that wrap around the neck, draw the eyes up. Add an empire waist to it and you are a force to be reckoned with.

———

SPAGHETTI-STRAP DRESS: Named so because of its thin straps, this style is dainty and delicate. Some are form-fitting, such as a sheath dress; whereas others are looser, such as a slip dress. Whatever you choose, throw on some wedge heels for a casual look or strappy heels for a little more pizzazz. Keep in mind that a thinner-strapped shoe adds a nice balanced look to this thin-strapped dress.

- **Booties and Hipsters:** Keep all eyes upward with strategically placed details and patterns. Start with a basic design that is cinched at the waist or tailored under the bustline. A gathered dress skirt is also a great starting point. A solid top and a boldly patterned bottom will keep the eye busy and looking upward. On a solid dress, such details as piping around the top, or belts sitting high on the waist will ensure that the focus is where you want it.

- **Dainties:** The lightness of the thin straps on a spaghetti-strap dress does not weigh down your petite stature. Rather, it provides lift and length. Showing skin on your arms, shoulders, back, and chest helps to elongate your frame and highlight your curves. Find one with a soft V-neckline to show even more skin. With a pair of sexy high heels, you'll look like a goddess.

- **Busties:** Think linguine or fettuccine rather than angel hair when it comes to picking your spaghetti-strap dress. A slightly thicker strap will help hold up the dress better under the weight of your breasts, and adjustable straps may give you extra length for a better fit. A style that crosses in the back may be the ticket to a little extra support. Unless the top of the dress is snug enough to hold you up on your own, you're going to need a strapless bra, or look for bras designed with clear straps.

- ***Belly Babes:*** Like Booties and Hipsters, you want the eye to wander upward, so start with a basic cut that is more tailored below the bust-line. If you are opting for something a little more form fitting, front ruching or layered fabric keeps that tummy looking taut. Otherwise, show off your zest for life with patterns, details, and shaped necklines.

Turn It Up, Tatas

You have so much flexibility when it comes to looking fabulous in dresses. Because a bra may not always be a necessity, play it up with halters, strapless, and spaghetti straps. Halter dresses with o-rings, twists or gathers at the bust will shape and show off your little lovelies. For more fullness up top, look for dresses with embellishments or details around the chest—such as spaghetti strap styles with bows, beading, or piping— or shirtdresses with pintucks or pockets on the chest. Tube dresses or smocked sundresses are also sassy choices for Tatas, especially when you're going for a Mia Farrow circa 1968 gamine vibe. Turn a few heads in a shift dress with a higher neckline and a hem that hits above the knee to accentuate your legs and create a foxy focal point. For nights out, slip on a backless dress for added sizzle and sex appeal—who needs cleavage!

WRAP DRESS: We absolutely love the wrap dress. Its fitted top and loosely flowing bottom flatters every figure. A wrap dress crosses under the bust, wraps through itself, and ties around the waist or the rib cage. For a more casual look, pair a wrap dress with ballet flats, mules, or kitten heels . . . or, jazz it up with stilettos or strappy sandals. Just about any shoe works with this dress, even boots (both flat and heeled—woo-hoo!). If that's not enough to make you love the wrap dress, the fact that you can adjust the ties and the

fit to work with your body will have you feeling like you've been struck by Cupid's arrow.

- ***Booties and Hipsters:*** The wrap dress loves curves. By hugging your upper half and flowing over your lower half, this style really defines your figure. The dress skirt should skim the bottom of your hips before flaring out a bit. This way, it flatters your backside while drawing attention down toward your lovely legs. The V-neck that naturally forms with a wrap dress will bring the eye upward. It's a perfect balance for you to keep the focus above and below your bottom and hips.

- ***Dainties:*** For you, dear Dainties, the layered V-neck of the wrap dress will give you a little more oomph up top. Because you hold the power in your hands with the sash or ties of the dress, add length with one that ties a little lower on the waist rather than around the rib cage. To create length from top to bottom, look for a vertical pattern or a dark, solid color.

- ***Busties:*** Busties in wrap dresses exude sexiness and class. The open neckline helps to balance your figure while showing off a little cleavage. With a large, heavy chest, the vertical and diagonal lines of this dress create openness and length from your neck down. The ability to tie this dress allows more give for an ample bosom. Look for a wrap that ties at your narrowest point—your waist. This will create space under your breasts, lengthening your torso and accentuating your curves (in a good way!).

- ***Belly Babes:*** Fabric is your best friend, so the layering of fabric afforded by the wrap dress is just what you need. The cut of this dress draws attention to curves and slims the midsection, so it is a great choice for you. Look for wraps that tie on the rib cage, a bit above the belly, to create a trimmer tummy. Big, bold patterns that move in a vertical direction further enhance the slimming effect.

———

STRAPLESS DRESS: Whether you are being whisked away to a black-tie affair or strolling through the park, the strapless dress has its place in every venue and with every body type. The difference between a cocktail and a casual strapless dress is in the details: fabric, styling, embellishments, and of course shoes. A gauzy, cotton strapless dress with flats versus a satin or taffeta strapless with stilettos is essentially the same garment, but "dressed" differently. The strapless also leaves you with a clean canvas to paint with jewelry, so bling it up with a necklace and a pair of earrings.

- **Booties and Hipsters:** A strapless dress that is fitted around the bust with a loose and flowing dress skirt to the knee will do wonders for your bottom half. The form-fitting top of the dress creates symmetry throughout your silhouette. Strapless dresses with sashes, belts, or gathers enhance the effect. By baring the wide lines of your shoulders in a strapless dress, you also have the added benefit of a natural balance between your upper and lower halves.

- **Dainties:** Lucky you! The strapless dress leaves Dainties with quite a bit of room for fun. From bustline to hemline, this style is essentially one long line, which works wonders for you. Of course, a solid color will have you looking taller, but don't shy away from patterns. A solid-color block around the bust, followed by a pattern with vertical movement on the bottom, might be just what you need. Also, keep the hemline around the knee and pair with heels, for a longer-looking leg.

- **Busties:** Despite what you may think, you can dazzle in a strapless dress. The reason being: skin. By baring your chest, shoulders, and arms, you create space that actually shows off your bosom without enhancing it. For you, the key to a strapless dress is support. A supportive strapless bra is usually a must with this type of dress, even if it already has a built-in shelf bra. Otherwise, you run the risk of sagging, or worse . . . monoboob! Keep them lifted and separated with a bra.

- **Belly Babes:** Play up those shoulders and arms and draw the attention north of the equator. Opt for a fitted top and a full skirt that flares above your hips. However, if you want a more streamlined silhouette, find a straighter cut with front details, such as ruched, gathered, or layered fabric. By creating volume over your midsection, you allow the fabric, rather than your tum-tum, to be front and center. Strapless sundresses whittle you away with their big and bold summer patterns.

EMPIRE-WAIST DRESS: The distinguishing factor of an empire dress is the high-cut waist. It usually sits below the bustline and above your natural waist. Because it is gathered higher than the waist, it creates a long and lean contour on virtually any body type, which makes the empire dress queen of the castle. You may want to make sure it has some shape, to avoid the question, "Oh! When are you due?"

- ***Booties and Hipsters:*** With the waistline raised above the natural waist, this style helps show off your assets. The fabric should flow graciously over your hips, bottom, and thighs rather than cling. You get the added benefit of the higher waist, which keeps their peepers peeking at your face and upper body. Pair this dress with stilettos or a thin, strappy shoe.

- ***Dainties:*** The longer skirt on an empire-waist dress makes this one a perfect pick for you. The longer panels of fabric draping from the high waist give the appearance of a lengthened torso. And, with details such as piping or layering around the neck and bustline, the eye is naturally drawn upward in a vertical direction.

- ***Busties:*** An empire-waist dress with a scoop, wide V-, or sweetheart neckline looks beautiful on Busties because the top is fitted. Simple clean lines in monochromatic colors around your chest will tame the bodaciousness below. Make sure that you have enough room in the top of the dress; an empire dress with a waistline that cuts through the center of your breasts is not so flattering. It needs to sit below, where it can taper you.

- ***Belly Babes:*** The raised waist on the empire dress is perfect for you. Not only does it taper in at a narrow point on your torso, but it also brings your top into focus, particularly when the neckline has piping, stitching, or some sort of structure to it. The draped part of the dress (below the high waist) should have a little gathering or texture to it, to keep it looking fluid.

TUNIC DRESS: The tunic may have its roots in ancient Greece and Rome, but it is a statement of fun fashion in today's modern world. Generally characterized by its straight, loose cut, the tunic dress presents itself with short or long sleeves, and most often hits the knee or thigh in length. Day or night, casual or cocktail, the tunic dress rules. It's adorable for day with ballet slippers, or spruced at night with high and happening heels. Because of its simplicity of form, you can get really creative with long necklaces and fabulous shoes.

- ***Booties and Hipsters:*** Keeping your upper body the focus, choose a tunic dress with a wide or boatneck, as it will help to balance your proportions. Because of the tunic's smooth lines, you won't be busied up with pleats or gathers. Instead of pockets, opt for bold patterns to spruce up your tunic. To maintain a long, lean line on your lower body, try a pair of tall boots with tights or stockings in a like color, or go bare and show your legs with some thin, strappy shoes.

- ***Dainties:*** Because the tunic is a clean dress with minimal fabric, you can really turn it up a notch! Keep it on the shorter side, to create length with your legs. If you are opting for tights or stockings, choose a hue that matches the base color of the dress and your shoes. This way, you will create continuity (and length!) from top to bottom. A long necklace that drops below your chest will add more vertical lines to your look.

- ***Busties:*** Break up your upper body with a wide V-, or boatneck dress. Balance it out with some low-sitting pockets on your tunic. They should be level with your hip bones so that you have enough distance between your bustline and the pockets to give you a pert and perky silhouette.

- ***Belly Babes:*** Who needs to do hundreds of crunches when you have a tunic to throw on? The loose-fitting hang of this dress keeps your tummy looking slim and trim. Look for one that has some shape to it, so that you don't swim in it; going too big and loose with this style can create the opposite of what you want. Along with fluid, low-contrast patterns, seek out a shorter hemline that falls just above the knee, to show off those lovely legs of yours.

FABULOUS FEMMES

Yasmine:

The first time we laid eyes on Yasmine, all we could say was *wow.* She is 100 percent woman—and every inch of her is Curvy to the max. Modern and exotic, sexy and proud, she can fill out a dress like nobody's business!

"I love vibrant colors because my skin color is café and bright greens (my favorite) or reds really make me stand out." Among her favorites are tie dresses that cross in the back and gather in the front to pull in more cleavage. "This string does two things: it really holds in my breasts so I don't spill out everywhere, and it flares open right under my breasts. Many women feel this style can make you look pregnant, but if it flares out beneath the breasts, it ends up looking flowing and feminine."

Another of Yasmine's knockouts is a fitted, curve-hugging black dress. The V-neckline plunges just enough to be tantalizing but not enough to be trashy. "The dress is very stuck to your body, so while it's very fitted, you're not showing too much skin. And, it hits right above my knees and follows my booty all the way through, which winds up accentuating it in a nice way."

Yasmine always pairs her dresses with a very high, often strappy pair of heels—and makes sure her legs are as divine as the rest of the package. "To make them look fabulous, I will spray a little Sally Hansen Airbrush on my legs to give them a glow."

Amy:

What we love about Amy is how she completely embraces her build. As a Tata, she proudly says: "I'm flat as a board and I *love* it because I can wear any type of top I want." That shows in her selection of dresses, which includes a variety of strapless styles (that you'd think would call for a little more something-something on top, but that doesn't stop Amy).

Whether she's going casual for the day in a funky sundress or stepping it up at night in a dressy black number, she takes full advantage of her tatas, shoulders, and long neck. She often wears very simple spaghetti-strap or strapless styles and then adds the wow factor by using scarves, necklaces, heavy bangles, or vintage clutch bags.

"My approach to cocktail dresses is to have three simple and versatile dresses that can be accessorized to look like thirteen dresses. How? Black, black and more black." Amy will pair black dresses with metallic jackets, dramatic bat-wing sweaters, long flapper beads, feathered scarves—and the combination always looks fresh.

"Because I'm the furthest thing from top heavy, I can wear anything." And she does!

Deena:

Deena is the quintessential dress girl. "They're so easy. It's one outfit; you don't have to think. And they're so versatile! Layer with tights and turtlenecks and throw on boots for winter, or wear during the summer with sandals, slingbacks, or wedges."

Deena decks out her delicious Dainty frame in long-sleeve shirtdresses, skirted vintage-style dresses, silk wrap dresses, or strapless cotton sundresses for summer—in other words, just about any style! She also loves to layer over dresses, whether it's a shrunken jean jacket or a fitted wrap cardigan.

"I recently realized I have more of a waist than I previously thought. The confusion is due to what I lovingly call 'the pooch' . . . a little, thanks to genetics, that threw me off for years until I discovered where my waist *really* is! So I've been trying to play it up a bit. I like the idea of having a curvy figure and emphasizing my hips and bum to look more curvy and feminine. I also like my neck and shoulders, and I have strong calves (after many years in high heels), so dresses show off all the good stuff!"

Taura:

Taura is a beautiful Busty (with the most stunning ice blue eyes). She loves color and *loves* to flaunt her figure in dresses. But, it's sometimes easier said than done. "Dress shopping is so frustrating . . . I find a cute dress, put it on, zip it up, and it usually only gets half way. But it fits beautifully everywhere else." She often ends up going a size larger so it fits her chest, and then she has the dress taken in to fit her back.

One sure bet for Taura is the halter dress. "I like ones that tie at the neck so I have control over how tight or loose it is. One problem I have with dresses is 'ho' syndrome. What looks cute and sweet on a smaller-bosomed girl can make me—a more amply bosomed lady—look like a ho!" But even in the face of adversity, Taura has learned how to dress her boobs, booty, and every inch of her bod flawlessly.

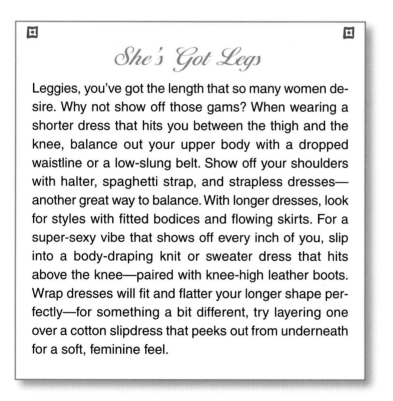

She's Got Legs

Leggies, you've got the length that so many women desire. Why not show off those gams? When wearing a shorter dress that hits you between the thigh and the knee, balance out your upper body with a dropped waistline or a low-slung belt. Show off your shoulders with halter, spaghetti strap, and strapless dresses—another great way to balance. With longer dresses, look for styles with fitted bodices and flowing skirts. For a super-sexy vibe that shows off every inch of you, slip into a body-draping knit or sweater dress that hits above the knee—paired with knee-high leather boots. Wrap dresses will fit and flatter your longer shape perfectly—for something a bit different, try layering one over a cotton slipdress that peeks out from underneath for a soft, feminine feel.

Michaela:

When asked about dresses, Michaela exclaims, "Ooooh, I love me a cocktail party! And I love a good dress." Specifically, she loves to deck out her Curvy frame in form-flattering wrap dresses, such as her ultimate fave, an orange and white Diane von Furstenberg. "I *love* the way I feel in this dress and the color pops against my skin tone. I think it's important to have one outfit, one dress that makes you feel like a *star*. I decided not long ago to buy only clothes that I feel *fabulous* in and that make me look fantastic." For more casual days, Michaela sometimes layers dresses over jeans. A belted shirtdress over a pair of dark denims, and a colorful pair of heels—it's a flawless, flattering look. Cheers, Michaela!

CHAPTER SIX

Loungy: Workout and Leisure Wear

Weekends, lazy afternoons, running errands, hitting the gym, and cozy nights at home . . . what better time to relax and do the things you love in the comfort of your softest duds. There's nothing better than slipping out of a blazer and pants and into your favorite pair of cotton sweats and a whispery light tee.

The best news is that loungewear has become much more modern and stylish—those bulky, oversized sweatsuits have been replaced by sophisticated athletic pants and zip-up jackets in techno fabrics that can be quite the showstoppers—so much so that you can even incorporate the pieces into your work attire on a casual Friday. As we like to say, it all comes down to how you pair.

So whether you're getting ready to hit the treadmill or snuggle up on the sofa with a bowl of strawberry gelato and a good flick, slip into something stylish *and* supercomfy.

Don't Sweat It!

HALL OF FAME

There's no way yoga pants couldn't make it into our Hall of Fame! It's the go-to piece of your weekend wardrobe that feels lush against your skin and supports your shape. Whether you wear this comfy staple to work out or a casual lunch with friends, it's a low-maintenance, polished look that easily transitions. Here's what you need to dash around town in leisure style: **dark, long, flared, roll-top, yoga-style pant**.

- *Dark.* Black, chocolate brown, and navy are versatile, figure-flattering neutrals. Look for medium-weight fabrics that hold you in and create a smooth line.
- *Long.* As with any type of pants longer = leaner.
- *Flared.* A shapely leg gives any body a more balanced look.
- *Roll-top.* This nifty design allows anyone from a Hipster to a Leggy to customize the fit on the belly.
- *Yoga-style.* Even if you don't indulge in "downward dogs," take advantage of the sleek booty-hugging silhouette, stretchy fabric, and feminine, curved leg.

FIT TO FLAUNT

When searching for lounge clothes, comfort is the first priority. But finding the right fit is just as important—who doesn't want to look sleek and sexy while relaxing on the sofa with a good book!

- Shop for soft, stretchy cottons and Lycra blends that are smooth against the skin and won't itch or irritate. Be aware of the weight of the fabric as well—mid-to-heavier-weight styles will contain and give a bit more coverage (including opacity) to your lower bod.
- Watch out for a crotch that is too snug (a.k.a. "camel toe") or a too-tight cut that rides up your butt. Go for a comfortably fitted look that doesn't exaggerate every crack and crevice.

- Most yoga pants tend to have breathable waistlines that allow you to move freely. Always check to make sure they don't cut into or bind the belly.

- Go for the most flattering length. Pants should hit at about midheel when worn with shoes. Most likely you'll wear them with sneakers, flip-flops, wedges, or ballet flats, so consider your shoe wardrobe as you shop.

WORKOUT/LEISURE 101

YOGA PANTS: We can't remember what life was like before yoga pants. They rank high in style and comfort and come in a variety of cuts to tickle most fancies, from extra long and cropped to capri and shin length. Stock up on them! The classic pair is designed with a stretchy roll top (or flat pull-on waist) and flared leg. We're fans of the drawstring versions, too, since you can customize the fit.

- *Dainties:* Full-length, roll-top styles designed with a stripe down the side will help elongate your figure. And, the roll top helps create curves. Cropped styles also work well on slender Dainties. A waist-defining tee or tank perfects the look.

- *Booties and Hipsters:* A fluid boot-cut with a drawstring waist will loosely hug your luscious thighs and hips and balance your body. Let the pants rest a little bit lower on the hip, for a sexy fit. On top, try a longer tee or tank that is fitted through the boobs and waist and flares at the hip.

- *Belly Babes:* The roll top is made for you. It helps support and hold the tummy in with the high waistband. Pair these pants with a fluid tee that is loose and banded at the bottom, ruched, or flared.

- *Leggies:* Yoga pants are ideal for your figure, and with those gorgeous gams you really can't go wrong with lengths or styles. Mix in a cropped pair for a little something different. A hip-length form-fitting stretchy racer-back tank or empire-waist tee is the finishing touch.

SWEATS: We're not talking about the sloppy old school ones with tight elastic at the ankle. The latest styles have a refined (not bulky) drawstring, and a similar design to boot-cut jeans. Plus, they come in lots of playful colors and fabrics, such as terry cloth, velour and cotton. You'll love coming home to them!

- *Dainties:* Fun colors can add some kick to your look and amp up your lower bod. Stick with form-fitted styles that won't overwhelm. Add a wedge flip-flop for extra height if you're in the mood. Go simple and fitted on top.

- *Booties and Hipsters:* The flair of the boot-cut leg helps to balance your hips and tummy. You may want to experiment with slightly wider leg styles for even more balance. Look for simple clean cuts in dark, solid colors. Thin vertical stripes down the side of the pants can give a more slimming look.

- *Belly Babes:* Sleek, fitted styles with a lower waist are the key for Babes. Go for lightweight fabrics that won't add bulk, along with drawstrings that lay flat against the belly. Pair with fluid hip-length tops with room to breathe.

- *Leggies:* You'll work it in a full-length flared leg with a lower-cut waist that balances your midsection. Pair with hip-length tanks or tees that skim the waistline.

Curve-alicious

Curvies, you'll feel comfy cozy in flare-leg sweats or yoga pants. Look for midweight fabrics that flatter your shape without weighing you down. Pair them with a ¾-length-sleeve tee with an empire waist, or a fluid V-neck tee that drapes against your skin (a top with a vertical design like a floral can help lengthen your torso). A hip-length zip-up jacket and casual espadrilles or wedge thongs complete the look.

TEES AND TANKS: Tees and tanks aren't just for sweating anymore. You can take your pick from an array of favorites—thermals, buttoned, playful patterns, bright colors, feminine tanks with built-in bras, and just about anything else you can think up. Don't be afraid to wear cute, feminine tees to the gym—you deserve to look good while you're working it. And feel free to toss on your "workout" tanks for weekend erranding—just zip on a hoodie or sweater and you're ready to roll.

- **Belly Babes:** Look for tops that are longer cut and empire waisted—they give you a bit of room while still offering a slimming and stylish (not baggy) silhouette. Ruched tees and tanks are another great pick. Belly Babes can rock in tees with long, flared arms—the slightly exaggerated shape nicely balances your upper and midbody. Pair more fluid or roomy tops with fitted pants for an overall look that is bodacious, not baggy.

- **Busties:** Look for V-neck tanks to balance your bust area. Pair them with long, zip-up hoodies for a bit more coverage, when you want it. Stick with simple patterns. Thermal tees with V-necks or scoop-necks can also wow. And halter-style tanks are brilliant for Busties, since they offer extra lift around the neck.

- **Tatas:** Layering tanks and thermals is the best look for your figure; it gives you shape but you're not swimming in it. Enjoy tanks with built-in support—lucky you, you can get away without wearing a sports bra. Look for loungy tops with a gathered or "crossover" bustline to beef up your boobs. And experiment with vibrant colors to give your upper bod some oomph!

- **Broads:** V-necks or low scoop-necks are a flattering choice for you since they elongate your upper torso. Wrap tops are also a smart look for beautiful Broads. And yes, you can wear racerback tanks—try longer cuts so that your vertical line stays long and lean.

ZIP-UPS, PULLOVERS, AND HOODIES: Choose from a yummy array of fabrics, such as velour, velvet, and knits, and an endless variety of colors. Today's hoodies and zip-up jackets are designed for a woman's body: form fitting, flattering, and accented with feminine touches. Long tanks underneath are the perfect way to layer. Let the tank peek out below to elongate your body and create slender lines.

Look for styles that are fitted through the torso and arms—zip-ups with Lycra or nylon blends and hoodies made of soft, lightweight cottons. Not only are they stylish but they leave endless possibilities for creating alluring looks—pair them with anything from yoga pants to cropped pants, sweats, and even your favorite jeans.

- *Belly Babes:* Try out traditional hoodie styles that have a single front pocket across the middle—it can provide a little extra (flattering) fabric in just the right spots. Zip-ups with ruched side detailing also do the trick.

- *Busties:* A zip-up works wonders on busty gals, since the zipper creates a natural (and very sexy) V-neck. Layer a low-cut neutral tank underneath

Strapped In

A trusty sports bra is a must. "Compression" styles work well on everyone—cut like a bandeau, they hold your boobies tight with thick, stretchy fabric. For added support, "encapsulation" styles are like an industrial-strength power bra. When shopping for a sports bra, racer backs and wide shoulder straps ensure a snug fit all over. Moisture-wicking fabrics help keep sweat from sticking to your body.

and a richer, darker-toned color for the top zip-up layer, to keep it all balanced.

- *Tatas:* Zip-ups with gathering around the bustline are both feminine and modern—a great choice for you. Wear over a gathered cami or tank with a fitted bustline.

- *Broads:* You can't lose with a long, fitted zip-up. Look for styles with a stand-up collar and vertical panels or designs, for an even more flattering fit. Try a V-neck tank or low scoop-neck tee underneath.

- *Dainties:* You'll love hoodies that boast side-slit pockets—they help create curves on a small frame. If you are petite (or a Booty/Hipster), zip-ups are the perfect top. The zipper creates a vertical line down your body, which means lean and long. Even when zipped, an elongating v-neck draws attention to all your best assets.

Playing Footsie

Lounging is all about treating your tootsies to low-maintenance, cool, and carefree footwear: flip-flops, slides, wedges, or funky sneakers. (Racing styles have much more pizzazz than your typical, bulky white athletic shoes—play up your look with a fun color, such as red, orange or green.) And when it comes to socks, slip on something thin and lightweight, such as Peds or a style that hits right at the ankle.

FABULOUS FEMMES

Britt:

True to her laid-back surfer lifestyle, Britt lives in loungy looks. Since she's always running between work, the gym, and the beach, she likes comfortable, easily washable clothes. Flare-leg, roll-top yoga pants and slim drawstring sweats are favorites because she's able to find them easily and at the right price. She's a big fan of coordinating them with extralong racer-back tank tops—just what she needs to flatter her five foot eleven figure. She loves the way the cut of the racer back accentuates her back muscles. Britt also buys a ton of men's white tank-style undershirts. As she says, "They get better every time you wash them, the price is so right, and when they get stained (with food and kid prints), I just throw them away and buy more!"

Tracey:

Tracey is a busy mom who's always on the go, so she needs comfortable, breathable clothes that are stylish, cute, and flattering. "I also like to wear clothes that can get dirty and then wash well after they have been worn." So loungewear is it!

With a small waist combined with muscular thigh and calves, she wears a lot of yoga pants (Tracey's an in-demand yoga teacher, too!) and two-piece track-style suits. "I wear all kinds of T-shirts, but mostly long-sleeve, V-neck, or scallop-neck that hits at the hips or just below." Yoga has blessed her with a jiggle-free figure (plus, she's long waisted) so she favors shirts that are cut long and snug, to show it off. She is also a big fan of layering—"I prefer to wear a tank top underneath my shirts"—it's a great way to add an extra layer of support and a bit of modern style.

CHAPTER SEVEN

Beachy: Swimwear and Cover-Ups

Aaah, summer. Days are longer, your skin has a nice, healthy glow about it, and everything just seems a little more laid-back. The bright sun warms your skin. Sand sifts through your toes. The cool, clear water laps at your feet. But with all of summer's glory also comes the often dreaded swimsuit season. Sometime around March or April, the stores start to fill their racks with those itsy-bitsy teeny-weeny polka-dot bikinis and we begin our long and sometimes laborious search for . . . a flattering swimsuit.

If you're one of those women who skulk past the swimsuit racks, fear no more. You can really turn it out during the summer months, whether you're picnicking on the beach or lounging poolside. Like everything in life, how you wear a swimsuit is all about attitude. Instead of buying one because you *must*, buy one because you love it!

With swimwear and beach attire, confidence is essential. And the key to confidence is a comfortable and flattering fit. That means no fussing and fidgeting while sunbathing on the sand. No worrying that your buxom boobs may spill out as you plunge into the pool. No pulling, tugging, and twisting.

Whether you sport a revealing string bikini or a glamorous one-piece, your swimsuit will reveal more of you than anything else you wear in public. So make sure it shows off every inch of you in the best light. Get your hunt on and go find that ever-elusive flattering swimsuit. Get rid of inhibitions, get to know what styles make you look and feel your best, and ring in the hazy days of summer in fearless style!

Swimmin' Sexy

HALL OF FAME

Long gone are the days when women wore wool tank suits with leg coverings that scandalously (and very unflatteringly) hit midthigh. Talk about full coverage . . . and a nasty farmer's tan! That was probably the last universal swimsuit style and we doubt anyone wants to revisit those days. While swimsuits are definitely an individual thing, there are a few styles that can flatter most figures. The tankini—a two-piece suit with a bikini bottom and longer tank top—is the most versatile swimwear style around and works wonders on all sizes and shapes. The tops come in cuts from bandeau to halter and can be worn longer or shorter, tighter or looser, to show off your midsection. Pair it with a scoop bottom and you have coverage along with unfettered femininity. To make a splash this summer, think: **dark, solid, adjustable, coverage, support, and details**.

- *Dark.* For a smooth and slim appearance, stick with dark colors such as black, navy, and chocolate brown. They are classics that make an appearance season after season. Plus, these tones have the added benefit of highlighting a great tan.

- *Solid.* To balance your silhouette, reach for a solid swimsuit. While prints may be eye-catching, they may also draw extra attention to areas you'd prefer keep a bit lower profile.

- *Adjustable.* The more adjustable the suit, the greater the opportunity for a perfect fit. Bottoms with side ties let you loosen or tighten when you need a little more or less breathing room in your bikini. And tops with ties and clips will definitely benefit your bust.

- *Coverage.* Not too much, not too little. Look for bottoms that cover your tush without sending it into hiding. Sometimes too much material on the booty and bust can enhance these areas, making them appear larger. On the other hand, not enough material and you look like the star of a "Girls Gone Wild" video. When it comes to tops, a good rule of thumb is to cover at least three-quarters of the bust.

- *Support.* There's no reason to let gravity steal the show here. Suits can lift and smooth in ways you might not realize. Underwires, ties, halters, tummy control, and special techno-fabrics are lovely little bonuses that are available with lots of today's styles.

- *Details.* Look for subtle extra details to add a bit of flair without being flashy. A simple tortoise shell ring, bust gathers, a touch of embroidery, appliqués, beading, or even a little burst of rhinestone bling can spruce up your suit. Whether you're looking for sass or sophistication, the devil is in the details.

Curves Ahead!

Want to create curves on your athletic build? For slender sassies with long, lean bodies and slim hips, it's all about the details. Ruffles, rings, belts, and bows placed on the hips create curves. A strapless bandeau or an over-the-shoulder bralette shortens the torso. One-piece suits that are belted, pinched at the waist, have side panels, are pleated, or criss-cross over the tummy will whittle your waist and create some kickin' curves.

FIT TO FLAUNT

Trying on swimsuits is something just about every girl dreads—it can be about as fun as a trip to the dentist (without the novocaine to numb you!). But you can transform a swimsuit shopping experience from painful to downright pleasant with the right approach and attitude.

- If you've spent the winter wrapped up in cozy cashmere or doused in down, chances are your silky skin suddenly exudes a certain pallor under the unforgiving fluorescent lights of the dressing room. Before trying on swimwear, get kissed by the "sun." Lather on some tanning cream, or sprinkle yourself with a spray tan for a bit of golden shimmer. The extra glow will help smooth your skin under the bright lights.

- Try on suits when you're not feeling bloated. During that time of the month or after a carb or salt binge, your body might be holding on to a little extra water. When you're stripping down for swimwear, you want to feel as light and airy as cotton candy. Consider flushing your system by drinking lots of water and eating light for several days before heading into the dressing room.

- At last . . . you think you've found the perfect suit, but the straps are just a little too long, or the bottom is a little too loose. Rather than tossing it back on the rack and starting from scratch, take it to the tailor. A pro can often make adjustments as needed—shortening or lengthening straps, inserting pads, gathering material, ruching, adding clasps, and reinforcing support are some of the ways swimwear can be altered. Just be sure you can return the suit before any alterations begin, in case the tailor can't do the fine-tuning. The extra money you spend on tailoring is worth it for a winning swimsuit!

- Few women are the same size on top as they are on the bottom. The swimwear goddess is looking out for those lovely ladies who might need a little more here and a little less there. Swimsuit separates have come to your rescue. Many stores now sell tops and bottoms separately, should your bubbly boobs not fit into the same suit as your tiny heinie.

- Jump up and down and wiggle all around. You may feel like you're doing the Hokey Pokey, but you're really checking to make sure nothing pops out or makes an unwanted appearance. The last thing you want when frolicking on the sand is a dreaded wardrobe malfunction.

SWIMWEAR 101

TWO-PIECE TOPS: Two-piece or not two-piece, that is the question. Halters, bandeaus, triangles, tanks, or some hybrid of styles . . . when it comes to swimwear tops there are so many choices it can make your head spin! Whatever your body type, there is a two-piece for you. Start with the right top and you've won half the battle . . . literally.

- *Busties:* Think support. For you buxom babes, it's all about lift. Halter tops provide great support, since the neck straps tend to be a bit wider while showing off that incredible cleavage. Look for tops with structured underbust bands for extra leverage. Bralettes with underwires and over-the-shoulder straps perform like a bra—supporting and lifting—but are camouflaged as swimwear. Busties can work a triangle top as long as there's enough coverage (at least three quarters of the breast) and the neck straps are wider for extra support. Being able to adjust the fabric width on a triangle top can work to your benefit. Also, straps that tie and adjust give you more flexibility, for a more personal fit.

- *Tatas:* You ladies can slip those perky pillows into pretty much anything. Triangle tops, bra-style tops, and bandeaus (particularly ones that have ties that start at the center of the cleavage and meet at the back of the neck) all work wonders for all you terrific Tatas. Go for embellishments, ruffles, ruching, and patterns to enhance the appearance of your chest. When looking for a pattern, try one that follows the natural contour of your breast. Many suits come with pads to add some cleavage, but underwire and boning can also do the trick. If you're small, think small— you lucky girls can champion the itsy-bitsy bikini top! Just remember, the less material, the better, otherwise you'll drown in all that fabric.

- *Belly Babes:* The tankini is your best friend—fun and flirty while providing a bit of extra coverage. Choose a length and looseness that you're comfortable in—cover your whole tum or show a sliver, or slip on a curve-hugging hip-length top or a floatier A-line. Experiment with halters, bandeaus, and over-the-shoulder styles to find one that expresses your personality while suiting your breast size and shoulder width. Being belly-licious in your bathing suit is easy when you choose tankinis with dark colors or ruching. Go as modest or as racy as you want—even max it out with slits on the sides or the back, for a bit of fun.

- *Broads:* For those of you blessed with beautiful, broad shoulders, balance them out with square lines and wide straps. Bandeau tops, tankinis, or bandeau tankinis with over-the-shoulder straps create a flattering box effect that streamlines your upper body. High-neck tops lengthen rather than widen, so they're also a good choice for you. Try a solid top matched with a print bottom, to draw the eye vertically. Such accents as belts, ties and sashes on your bottom show everyone that you've got it goin' on.

TWO-PIECE BOTTOMS: Some are round. Some are flat. Some are bubbly. Some are wide. Some are perky. Some are jiggly. Love 'em or leave 'em, we all got a bottom—and no matter what type you have, someone is diggin' it! Women have launched careers off their derrieres—a testament to the power of the posterior. So this summer, when you pull that two-piece bottom over your caboose, breathe a sigh of relief knowing that it will bask in its glory as well as the sun.

- *Booties and Hipsters:* The saying, "less is more," suits Booties and Hipsters to a tee. Extra fabric can actually enhance your bottom and hips, whereas a high-cut leg can be very slimming. For full coverage in front and back, consider the scoop bottom. It covers the booty without hiding it and flatters your curves. The scoop bottom sits below the belly button and shows just enough hip to lengthen your legs. If you want to show a little more skin, try a hipster bottom, which sit a little lower on the hips while still covering your backside. Keep the bottoms dark and solid and if you want a pattern, find one with single-block colors or large prints.

- *Leggies:* You are the blessed babes who can wear boy shorts flawlessly. Your long legs are perfectly suited for these straight-cut bottoms that ride low on the waist and across the hips. Skirtinis are miniskirted bikini bottoms, and like boy shorts, they really add some curve to slender hips. For summer sweetness, find one that is smooth and short and sits flat like a tennis skirt. Or turn the heat up a notch with string bikini bottoms. Looking for something in between? Try hipster bottoms. Embellishments like belts, rings, ties, and bows, small patterns, and bright colors allow you lovely Leggies to let loose.

- *Dainties:* Whether demure or daring, there is a two-piece bottom that is right for you. You want to think length. Vertical stripes or a solid bottom paired with a printed top work wonders for you. Hipster bottoms are a surefire way to elongate your torso by creating more space between your top and bottom. If you want to lengthen your gorgeous gams, high-waist bottoms tend to have a higher leg opening, which creates a longer look. An added plus: they also whittle your waist.

- *Belly Babes:* Tie bottoms give Belly Babes the flexibility to make adjustments as needed for a smooth, comfy fit. You want the fabric on the front of the tie bottoms to rest flush across your midsection without creating any pooch. Boy shorts fall below the stomach, which can work to your advantage, as they don't cut into the center of your tummy. Pair them with a longer tankini top for a luscious look. Dark colors, large patterns and textured fabrics will give Belly Babes just the right punch!

———

ONE-PIECE SUITS: Even though the one-piece offers more coverage, don't underestimate it! It can be just as sexy as the two-piece and the right one-piece shows off the back, cleavage, and thighs just enough to pique curiosity. If you're a water sports lover, a one-piece also gives much needed support. As long as it lays flat on the bottom and rests firmly but not tightly around the shoulders, you should feel safe taking the plunge off the high-dive. Suit up with a hot one-piece and tons of confidence, and you'll be swimmin' in style.

- **Curvies:** Show off those curves! One-piece styles suit you perfectly. A deep V-neckline, classic maillot suit or halter in rich, dark colors will flatter your shapely silhouette. Turn it up a notch with a higher cut leg to slim and lengthen your look. A little Lycra can also go a long way when it comes to swimwear, providing tummy control and side support. Add some long, vertical side panels and you'll be burning up the beach. If you're looking for a little extra coverage, try a blouson—a one-piece with a flowing tank top that ties at the waist. Want to reveal a little skin? Try a version with subtle cut-outs and mesh inserts—with just the right placement, these extras can bring out the best in your kickin' curves.

- **Booties and Hipsters:** Be bold and show off your personality with patterns and prints—along with dark colors, they will slim your silhouette. And, why not mix it up a bit—try a one-piece suit with a solid bottom and printed top. Bring the focus upward with detail at the bustline. Wide straps and a strong neckline will also help balance your figure. Any suit with an emphasis on the top, such as a maillot or halter, will draw the eye up while leaning and lengthening your frame. A boatneck or racer-back suit will bring the emphasis to your shoulders and create a flattering figure. For the modest miss, try an empire-waist swimdress, which covers a bit more of your bum while drawing attention to your top.

- **Busties:** Support. Support. Support. Shall we say it again? A variety of one-piece styles with structure up top is available for the bustiest of Busties. Underwires, soft foam cups, or shelf bras all provide what you need during swimsuit season. Anything that gives you some lift will have you turning heads. Look for something that elongates your chest. Halters, scoop necks, and V-necks, as long as you can find one with (what's the magic word?) support, will all show off your cleavage and lengthen the space from your neck to your bust. Go for broader and structured straps rather than thin and string straps, since they will hold the weight of your breasts and be more comfortable against your shoulders. Adjustable straps give you the flexibility you need for a customized fit. If minimizing is your mantra, wide-set straps, a big all-over pattern, or a crossover/surplice-style top (which wraps across your body) is your calling.

- **Belly Babes:** Dive right in to the swimsuit search and experiment with styles that express your personality. Big and bold prints (think florals, swirls, and animal prints), centered ruching, criss-crossing under the bust, vertical or diagonal stripes, and bust details such as rings offer you many options—the hardest part will be deciding which one you like the best. Many suits now come with tummy control and side panels, making a suit comfy while expertly trimming your midsection. If you're feeling really troubled by your tummy, flaunt your bottom and bust. High-cut legs help to taper your waistline. Match them with wide-set straps on top and work your heavenly bod. Look for cuts that bring attention to your bust, such as the halter, scoop neck, or maillot top. A crossover or surplice-style one-piece will also drape over your tummy. For the ultimate find, look for one that gathers as it wraps around your waist and blends into the suit.

Turn It Out, Tatas

It's one thing to go swimming in a suit—another thing to swim in one. When it comes to a one-piece, your tatas don't have to wade in pools of fabric. A one-piece with some design on top will keep your peaches looking plump. A halter or bandeau top that's gathered at the cleavage or has embellishments such as rings can help. For a little extra oomph, there's always padding and underwires.

This Ain't Your Mother's Muumuu

HALL OF FAME

Toss out those old cut-off shorts and wrinkled tanks, and grab something with a little more flair instead. Dressing for the beach or pool means more than just throwing on a swimsuit. Shake things up with a sassy cover-up. You take so much time and effort searching for the right suit, so don't let it get lost under a baggy, raggy T-shirt. A good cover-up hits a happy medium between covering and baring it all. It's the must-have little number to throw on when you need to grab a bite from the snack shop or run to the girl's room. The perfect style is: **a longer tunic that is soft, fluid, airy, and fitted**.

- *Longer.* Tops and dresses that land somewhere just below the bottom to the middle of the thigh will cover your hips, booty, and thighs while still letting you show some leg. It's also a good landing mark to balance out your top half.

- *Tunic.* With various necklines, shapes, and sleeve lengths, the tunic style is an all-around crowd-pleaser. And, it drapes your body for a flowing, fabulous fit.

- *Soft.* If you're doing some major basking and baking, it feels a lot more soothing to wear something that caresses your skin. Such materials as gauze, terry cloth, and light jersey weaves feel cool and soft when covering up.

- *Fluid.* A cover-up that falls loosely from your body will highlight your curves rather than indulge the bulge. Look for a top, dress, or skirt that has movement in the materials.

- *Airy.* Light, breezy materials, such as crocheted cotton and gauze, let the air pass through, feel nice against the skin and help keep those sticky summer oils and lotions at bay.

- *Fitted.* Styles that are slightly fitted at the waist with a bit of a flare at the bottom or slits on the sides will add shape to your beautiful bod.

FIT TO FLAUNT

The difference between looking fabulous and looking frumpy at poolside can sometimes come down to whether your cover-up fits. Go for styles that are loosely fitted—you don't want to be swimming in it!

- When trying on cover-ups, pull them on and off several times. Are they easy to get into and out of? The transition from cover-up to swimsuit should be effortless. The last thing you want to do is struggle with your cover-up at a crowded beach or pool.

- Rotate your arms, lift your legs, squat down, stretch your chest. No, this isn't pure power aerobics. You're just checking for ease of movement in your cover-up. Since you'll probably throw it on for a stroll down the beach, run to the snack shop, or even a game of smash ball, you want to make sure you can easily move in it.

- Try it on with your swimsuit. Since a cover-up complements your swimwear, they should look good together. Bring your swimsuit to the store or make sure you can return the cover-up in case it doesn't match.

- Chest, bum, and tum: make sure the cover-up gives you breathing room in these areas. While you want it to be fitted, you don't want it to pull. A little room goes a long way.

- Because a cover-up can provide extra protection from the sun on those days when you've overbroiled, check to see that it covers enough skin while still feeling light enough to keep you cool. That way, you can keep having fun in the sun without overexposing your skin.

COVER-UPS 101

CAFTANS AND TUNICS: The caftan or tunic comes in so many styles that you can easily find one to rock your bod. V-necks, boatnecks, long, short, and varying sleeve lengths make the tunic a versatile top. Find one that flows with your body and you'll be sauntering in the sun.

- *Busties:* For the Busty beach babe, look for a lower-cut tunic to lengthen the space between your neck and chest.

Show off your collarbone and cleavage with a scoop, boat or V-neck-line. The cut should taper in at the waist and end with a slight flare or detail at the hemline. This will balance your bustline and create an hour-glass look.

- **Tatas:** Work that tunic, Tatas. Blouse it up a bit with a belt or tie, to add movement to your upper half. Long or 3/4-length sleeves with a slight flare will also balance your upper bod. Square- and deep V-neck tunics on tempting Tatas will turn heads.

- **Belly Babes:** The tunic was made for you. Go for big, fun designs that really pop. Find one that shows off your chest and hips but is slightly tapered at the waist. Slits on the bottom give you extra breathing room and show off those gorgeous gams.

- **Broads:** Square-necked tunics are magic on you. Look for one that is flared or slit at the bottom to create balance with your top half. Vertical stripes or graduated colors that go from dark on the top to lighter on the bottom will create a shapely transition down your torso.

––––––––––

KIMONOS AND ROBES: The kimono or robe is really one of the easiest cover-ups to slip in and out of, sliding on and tying at the waist. It's a no-brainer, and we love that! They come in different lengths and usually have 3/4- to full-length sleeves. It's also a sweet way to let your swimsuit top peek through.

- **Busties:** This is the style for you because it generally has a deeper cut and angled front that elongates and opens up your chest. The tie feature on these cover-ups draws in your waist and minimizes your bust. A wraparound ki-mono cover-up will really work the lines and curves of your body.

- **Tatas:** With the kimono draped over your swimsuit, you'll create a layering effect that makes those tatas pop. Let your swimsuit top peek through, for added volume. A patterned or light swimsuit top poking out from under a solid or dark cover-up will cause a sizeable scene.

- **Belly Babes:** The side-tie or wrap-style kimono creates a tapered waistline on Belly Babes. The extra fabric and layering of the wrap over the tummy is superflattering on you. If you go for a front tie, bunch up the fabric in front. Big, swirling patterns make for a perfect finish.

- *Broads:* To elongate your body and create a vertical line, a front-tie kimono or robe worn loose in the front will give you added length and balance and let your bikini or one-piece take center stage.

————

TERRY CLOTH: Whether you're in the mood for a dress, hoodie, tank, or miniskirt, terry cloth is made for pool- or ocean-side. We love that terry is absorbent, it's really useful if you're still a little damp from lounging in the water.

- *Busties:* This one leaves you with quite a few options. A bandeau terry dress worn over a halter-top swimsuit looks just right, as long as you find one with a bandeau wide enough to cover the length of your breasts. A terry miniskirt worn low on the hips elongates the torso between your breasts and hips, and helps give your chest a natural lift.

- *Tatas:* A cap-sleeve style with extra detailing adds width to your upper body and creates more curves. The bunched elastic and fabric on a bandeau-top terry dress gives you a lift. Find one with neck ties that start at the cleavage or with extra detailing such as bows.

- *Belly Babes:* The nappy terry cloth fibers give you a natural textured look. Halters, hoodies, tanks . . . pretty much anything works for you, as long as it tapers at the waist and leaves room to move. Miniskirts that sit low on the waist keep the tummy smooth rather than cut into it.

- *Broads:* To create a long, vertical look, try a terry dress with a high neck. Sleeveless dresses (*oh*-so-cute with a zip-front and a hood) lead the eye up and down your frame. Any type of dress with a square neckline, such as a bandeau, will balance your shoulders with your hips. Let those straps from your swimsuit make an appearance, and look dishy from head to toe.

T-SHIRT DRESS: We love our T-shirts. They're soft and comfy and there's nothing better than cozying up in one after a long day at the beach. Between V-, scoop, round, crew, and boat-necks, along with varying hem and sleeve lengths, the combinations are endless. A good rule of thumb is to follow the style of your favorite T-shirt. Keep the fabric light and you'll be the summer sizzle.

- *Busties:* As always, V-necks are made for you whether on land or at sea. You can get a little risqué when it comes to a V-neck T-shirt dress and really let it plunge, since your swimsuit will already be covering your breasts. Otherwise, a more modest V- or scoop-neck that highlights your collarbone and part of your chest will create openness. A dress that is a bit fitted rather than baggy will show off your waist and minimize your chest.

- *Tatas:* You can pretty much wear any cut when it comes to a T-shirt dress. A high boatneck dress will create width and length over your chest, since it spans from shoulder to shoulder, broadening the upper body. An off-the-shoulder T-shirt dress with details such as bows or ruffles creates the look of a bigger bosom.

Baby Got Back

Booties and Hipsters, whether you sport a tunic, a tube dress, or anything in between, find a cover-up with a tapered waist and a flare at the hem. Details around the bust will draw attention up, up, and away. An empire-cut cover-up or one with a structured top will also bring the line of vision upward. Remember, loose and flowing are the way to go. You want to feel light and airy as if you could float away.

- **Belly Babes:** Any T-shirt dress that tapers in at the waist and boasts a bit of a flare at the hem will bring out your inner hourglass . . . particularly those with scoop or V-necks that draw attention to your upper body. A jersey knit with some texture to it, such as loose ribbing, will put your belly in its place. At the other end of the spectrum, a super blousy dress that comes together at the bottom with a drawstring or tie is a fresh look that lets Belly Babes bring it on.

- **Broads:** Go sleeveless. A wide-strapped tank dress or sleeveless T-shirt dress will create vertical lines from your shoulders. Any T-shirt dress with a high neck or detail that wraps around the neck, such as a collar or straps, will create a long, narrow look for your upper half.

———

SARONG: The sarong or pareu is probably the most versatile of the cover-ups. Depending on the length and width of it, you can wear it as a long or short skirt, or as a dress. Take a hint from the Polynesians, who have worn these for centuries and have mastered the art of wrapping the soft, sheer fabric around their tanned torsos. There are dozens of ways to wrap a sarong, so let your imagination flow.

- **Busties:** The most obvious way to wear a sarong is tied around your hips, and Busties, this look suits you perfectly. Wear it as a long skirt or a short one, and play with different ties or knots. The distance created between your bathing suit top and the skirt helps create a sleeker bustline. Stylish sarong clips made from natural materials such as shell and wood will keep it securely tied. Wrapping a sarong around your upper body and then twisting the edges to make a tie around your neck creates a very flattering halter effect to keep you looking busty and beautiful.

- **Tatas:** Have fun experimenting with different ways to make a dress out of your sarong. A simple look that creates a commotion around your cleavage is to wrap the sarong around your upper body and under your arms. Grab the edge of fabric a few inches away from your body and tie the two sides together. The end result is a large knot at your bust with long, tapered fabric flowing down the front. You can also try various over the shoulder ties or toga wraps.

- ***Belly Babes:*** Sarongs are a great way to take the focus off the belly. With their bright patterns and colors, they can flatter anyone. When wrapping one as a skirt, let it rest on your hips and tie it firmly without making it so tight that it cuts into your abdomen. Making one into a dress gives you several options, as well. You can wrap it around your body as you would a towel, tie it to the side of your cleavage, and let it drape loosely over your center or try different neck ties to create length.

- ***Broads:*** You'll love the versatility of the sarong. Wrap the sarong as a dress around your upper body and tie the corners around your neck to create a halter. The edges will fall in layers down your front for a long, lean look.

FABULOUS FEMMES

Barbara:

Barbara's mantra is, "I will wear any suit that fits." Because she has a larger top half, she prefers to buy suits as separates. She loves to shop at Everything But Water and does well with the Shoshanna brand, since many of the tops are designed to flatter bustier girls. Bra-style tops with underwire and padding is her thing. And her mantra is "skin to win, baby!" so she loves to show it off against bright colors such as turquoise blue. Then again, she loves her simple black Speedo racer-style suit just as much—"It makes me look and feel powerful because it really shows off my shoulders and back." Go for it, Barb!

Britt:

Since she's a year-round surfer and swimmer, Britt is very hard on her suits. She refuses to buy a hundred-dollar bathing suit that will be roughed up and dry rotted in a couple months. So, Old Navy is Britt's first stop for bathing suits. All she needs is a colorful sporty suit that she can move in. She likes halter bikini tops because they provide a little more support, and bottoms with sides that tie so she can adjust them depending on her level of activity. When sunbathing, she finds it more flattering to tie them just enough to gently rest on her hips (so they don't dig in). While surfing, Britt makes sure her suit fits nice and snug, so she doesn't have any "indecent exposure moments."

Tracey:

Tracey's approach to swimsuits is simple: "I wear what looks good and is comfortable and user friendly in the water." That usually means a two-piece with a bra-style or tankini top—styles that work well on her body because she's a bit of a Busty. These types of tops offer good support, and they're comfortable and stylish as well.

Thanks to daily yoga workouts, Tracey's tummy doesn't reveal the fact that she's a mom. So she can flaunt it in low-waist bottoms that show a little skin—in *front*. As far as the backside, she makes sure to keep the tush "completely covered."

CHAPTER EIGHT

Lacy: Bras and Undies

Nothing on earth can make us feel instantly sexier than a delightfully demure bra and the laciest panties. Sometimes it seems such a shame that no one gets to see them! But once you've covered your undies up with all sorts of layers, you may start to feel like what you're wearing underneath doesn't matter so much . . . Nothing could be further from the truth!

Bras and undies are the foundation pieces of a great wardrobe and a great look. No matter how big or small your boobs are, they need the right support. And the right bra also provides extra enhancements—a little lift, a bit more size, or just the right amount of cleavage. Meanwhile, the right pair of underwear will preserve and protect the beauty of your booty. No wrinkles, no bubbles, no bulges.

In the end, boost your confidence with those little somethings that you slip into at the beginning. Slide on a feather-light thong, wiggle into a silky boosting bra, and anything you put on top will say *"thank you!"*

Babes in Bra-land

HALL OF FAME

A stroll through the Lingerie department can be so dizzying—bras come in more colors, patterns, sizes, and styles than we ever dreamed of. There's padded, soft cup, demi cup, underwire, racerback, wide straps, thin straps, clear straps, silk, satin, cotton, lacy, plain, pretty, playful, and any other personality to suit your perky boobs. Not only that, a bra can easily cost more than the shirt you're wearing over it!

While we'd love to simplify the selection, there's no way to narrow this all down to one bra that will work for every shape. But whether your tastes are plain-jane or frilly-and-fancy, there is one basic wear-with-anything bra that you should consider making part of your undie wardrobe . . . **molded— skinny, simple, silky, and neutral.**

- *Molded.* A molded cup gives you the coverage you need—no nips, no sagging. Busties will want to go with an underwire version, while Tatas can look for soft molded cups. Either way, you've got the support you need.
- *Skinny.* Thinner straps tend to be a bit more stylish and versatile. You want them just wide enough so that they won't dig in and be uncomfortable but thin enough so that you can wear them with a variety of tops.
- *Simple.* It's best to stick with simpler styling for your everyday basic bras. No seams and no lacy layers to peek through or create bumps and bulges.
- *Silky.* Silky or satiny bras tend to create a smoother look under clingy tops and tees.
- *Neutral.* Keep it neutral: creams, nudes, and blacks are the workhorse colors that you can wear with anything and everything.

FIT TO FLAUNT

It's one of the most important foundation pieces and yet, funnily enough, so many of us walk around in a bra that just doesn't quite fit. If you're not sure if you're a 34D or a 36C, head to the pros and that trusty measuring tape.

- Finding a bra that really, truly fits the way it's supposed to begins with knowing what size you really, truly are. You can try to measure yourself using rather complicated formulas that you find online or in books, but none of them are foolproof. We recommend that you head to a local specialty boutique or the lingerie section of your favorite department store to let a professional measure and assess your size. Nordstrom and Victoria's Secret both offer this service free of charge, so take advantage.

- If the band of a bra is too tight around your chest, you'll obviously need to try a larger size—going, say, from a 32 to a 34. But since that larger size may affect the overall fit, try going down a cup size to compensate—if that doesn't work then go back up another cup size.

- Your breasts should fill the cups without spilling out or bulging. Cleavage is a beautiful thing, as long as the bra is still comfy.

- It's not a bad idea to take along a few different tops when shopping for new bras—a wider neck (like a boatneck), a deep V-neck, a sheer blouse. This way you can see how it might work with a variety of cuts and determine whether you need a more revealing cut, more coverage, more support, etc.

- Lingerie doesn't have to be super pricey, but good bras are a worthy investment. Check local discount stores for affordable basic bras, then if you want, you can splurge now and then on a frilly little something to spice up your wardrobe of "unmentionables"!

BRAS 101

SOFT CUP: Flexible and super comfy, soft cup bras are a great everyday choice for gals who can do with a minimum of support. No underwires, no padding, just the basics. This style can get the job done well well—especially for A and B cups—so it's a winner in our bra book.

- **Busties:** Soft cups may be a bit challenging for Busties, but if you experiment with this style, your best bet is a soft cup that provides fuller coverage and isn't cut too low.

- **Tatas:** Try a very simple triangle style or one with an elasticized band under your bust to avoid the "shelf" effect that some more structured bras can give.

MOLDED CUP: Just what it sounds like: a bra featuring molded cups that gives your boobs a smooth and natural look. They can be soft cup or underwire. You may also hear the term "contour bra" which is a molded style containing a light lining of fiberfill or foam.

- *Busties:* Underwire molded bras are a wonderful option for you. Contour bras can help to contain and shape your boobs.

- *Tatas:* Choose a wireless version . . . and if you're in the mood, contour bras can provide a little extra oomph.

———

UNDERWIRE: Since the job of a bra is to support, nothing does it quite like an underwire. It lifts and gives perk to even the most ample bosoms, and has near magical powers to create cleavage. Whether full or demi-cup style, underwires offer over-the-top sexiness plus support.

- *Busties:* Look for fuller cups that will give your "girls" the coverage they need.

- *Tatas:* Slip on a demi-cup bra—a divine way to showcase your tatas!

To Pad or Not to Pad

Padded bras sort of offer a mini boob job in an instant—if and when you feel you want a bit of extra oomph. They can take you up a cup size and give your tatas a beautifully defined full, round shape. Just remember that less is more when it comes to padding, so that you don't start to look overinflated.

CAMISOLE: The camisole is the bra's pretty, popular cousin. A must for layering under sweaters and anything sheer, camis can be at once innocent and ultra-sexy. Stock up on styles from form-fitting scoop-necks to lacy V-necks, and enjoy the comfort that comes with wearing a camisole. Also, the good news for gals of all shapes and sizes is that camis offer plenty of variations, so you can customize the fit based on how much support you need.

- *Busties:* Look for camisoles with built-in bralettes (which come in either a soft support style or a more serious "bra" design for bustier babes).

- *Tatas:* Look for stretchy fabrics that will cling to your bod and your boobs; nylon or cotton blends with a dose of Lycra will do the trick, and your tatas will have the snug fit they need.

Pretty Panties

HALL OF FAME

Thank goodness we live in the age of pretty panties! There was a day when thick white cotton granny undies were the style du jour. Still, with the many choices available, picking a Hall of Fame was easy. When it comes to a pair of panties that fits every single body shape under the sun, it's all about the *thong.* If you haven't tried one, you don't know what you're missing. For perfect fit every time, slip on a thong—**simple, light, low-cut, and neutral.**

- *Thong.* The butt-crack styling of a thong may not seem like the most comfy thing, but it doesn't feel like you have underwear on at all. And you immediately do away with any dreaded VPL, bulges, or bulk.

- *Simple.* Regardless of what you're going to wear over it, simple undie styles tend to be a best bet: without a lot of heavy lace or other stuff going on to make it feel bunchy or scrunchy.

- *Light.* Ultra-light fabrics like meshy nylons or whispery light cottons are the way to go—they work well with thongs and ensure that the fit is really "barely there."

- *Low-cut.* Slightly low-cut is fine (it doesn't have to be down to *there* . . .). You want to maximize what you can wear a pair of panties with, and low-cut allows you to sport your low-waist denims or low-slung skirts without the fear of your skivvies peeking out.

- *Neutral.* As with bras, neutral colors are the basics that will get you through day to day: cream, nude, and black.

FIT TO FLAUNT

Whether you fancy thongs or full-cut briefs, the key with panties is to choose styles that are pretty and practical. Pretty because it just feels good, and practical because you don't want any bunching or binding to get in the way of a glamorous getup.

- Take several pairs of pants (and skirts if you like) along when trying on undergarments. It's a good idea to take along your trickiest item— whether it's a pair of white jeans or a slim pair of slacks—to ensure that whatever you choose remains invisible.

- Check for binding around the butt, thighs, and tummy. No matter how in love you are with a certain style, if it cuts into any of these areas, then it's not the right fit. Don't be shy about going up a size (*who cares!*)—the main thing is to be comfortable since panties are the base of any outfit.

- Experiment with different fabrics to see what feels best against your skin. Sometimes cottons are the coziest . . . other times silks feel more smooth and subtle. And today's microfiber marvels have practically reinvented the whole idea of wearable, breathable undies.

PANTIES 101

THONG: Comfy beyond compare. Wearable with anything. And so kind to our bums—we love the way a thong just let's our derrieres hang out and be booty-ful . . . Need we say more? Booties and Hipsters can look for higher-cut legs and ultra-light fabrics that don't bind at the hips. Check out styles (like Hanky Panky) that feature wider backs that lie flat and smooth. Belly

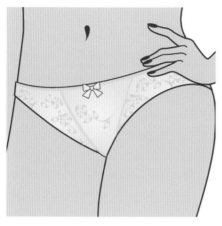

Babes will do well with thongs that hit mid-tummy and, again, ultra-light fabrics that don't bind and create bulge. Leggies should try out styles that cut a bit lower on the hip to balance out the leg line. Finding a flattering thong isn't hard, so don't sweat it!

———

BIKINI: The all-time, all-girl classic. Bikinis are a favorite pick when you want low-cut style but a little more rear coverage than a thong offers. They're great with short skirts or minis as well as with pants that are a little roomier in the rear. Stick with very light stretchy fabrics like mesh to avoid any sliding or bunching. Booties and Hipsters will do well with string bikini styles, with medium-width straps that won't bulge but also won't slice into you. Belly Babes will do well with bikinis that hit a little higher on the tummy. And Leggies, again, may want to opt for a bikini strap that hits mid-hip to even out proportions.

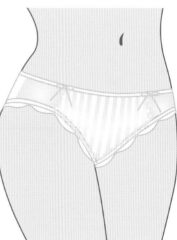

———

BRIEF: Briefs combine the extra tummy tucking that we sometimes want with a little old-fashioned girly flavor. Fortunately, designs have come a long way, so these aren't your granny's briefs! With lacy details and high-cut legs, briefs can still show off our curves in all the right ways while giving you maximum coverage fore and aft. Belly Babes may want to check out styles that feature tummy-firming panels. Hipsters will love high-cut briefs that accentuate the waist while leaving hips unencumbered. Booties will do well in styles that hit a bit lower in the backside and offer firm coverage that isn't stiff (in other words, doesn't cut into your rump).

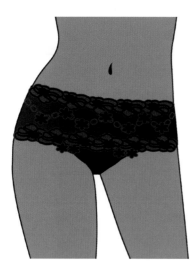

BOY-CUT: The perfect combination of funky and feminine, boy-cut briefs show off the belly, accentuate the hips, and give your curves a playful kick. Slim Dainties and Leggies will find big-time flattery with this style. Belly Babes, Booties, and Hipsters can slip into an ultra-light boy-cut made from an airy netted nylon or super-sheer synthetic—the best way to avoid VPL! Keep it light and just barely fitted. Boy-cuts are best under looser-fitting skirts and loungy pants, and since they basically look like modified hotpants, they're great any time you think your undies might show a bit. They're also a bedtime favorite, so stock up on a few colorful cotton pairs and sweet dreams!

Slimmers and Shapers

Every now and then we feel as if we could use a little lift here or a tiny tuck there to perfect our lusciously curvy figures. That's where shape-shifting undies come in, offering support under our favorite body-skimming dresses and fitted pants. Available in versions from briefs to full-body bustiers, they lift the bum, smooth the thighs, and pull in our pooch with stretchy spandex control panels. So instead of sucking it in, just tuck it in to one of these miraculous undergarments.

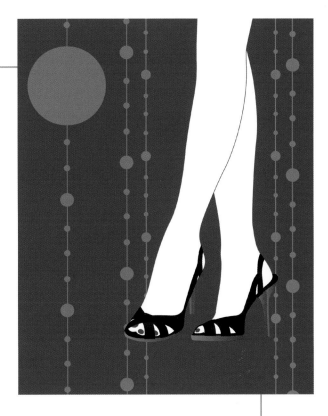

CHAPTER NINE

Shoes and Extras

Once you've got the basics of your wardrobe down, it's time to add those not-so-little extras. Shoes, bags, jewelry, and accessories can literally transform an outfit—and flaunt your figure in ways that might surprise you!

Shoes are the ultimate way to dress up (or down) any look, grow a few inches, add vintage flair, play with color, experiment with fashion, and make a dramatic statement. Like Dorothy in the Land of Oz, shoes are our magical meal ticket. Aside from the endless varieties, what we love about shoes is how easy they are to work with (no worrying about how they flatter your tum or beautify your bum). Whether you're a sneakers-and-sandals girl or wild about wedges, discover the many ways shoes can shake up your wardrobe.

Bags are not just a fashion accessory . . . they're an obsession! Leather, suede, studded, sweet and simple—bags allow us to add color, sophistication, sass, or a bit of bohemian flair. A versatile handbag wardrobe could include several neutral daytime bags (black, brown, tan, maroon), a go-anywhere weekend tote, a couple of evening clutches, and anything else that tickles your fancy. We feel the same way about bags as we do about shoes: you can never have too many of them!

And from casual to couture, no look is complete without what we like to call the icing on the cake—jewelry, hats, scarves, belts. A long, layered necklace can take a plain dress from drab to divine. A colorful scarf can make an outfit. While these are often the last pieces we put on, they are some of the most important!

Whether it's a simple pair of hoop earrings or a pair of knee-high black leather boots, we're always amazed at how accessories can flatter our figures. A pair of sparkling earrings can brighten your face and slim your neck. A dangling drop necklace can play up your cleavage and accentuate the vertical line of your body for a slimming effect. A pair of nude-colored heels can make your legs appear longer, while a pair of bright red peep-toes can draw attention to your lower bod and balance you out in wondrous ways.

Anyway you cut it, those little finishing touches have a huge impact!

SHOES 101

PUMPS: One hundred percent feminine and a great look for work or play. Slip them on with straight skirts, flat-front pants, or straight-leg jeans. The perfect pump comes down to shape—a slightly curved and slender heel, an elegant slope, and a refined toe. Subtle details like two-tone, small bows, or cutouts at the toe can add interest without going overboard. A favorite for everyone from Leggies to Hipsters, pumps give us a high dose of the "long and lean" look when we crave it.

WEDGES: If you're in the mood for some height but with a more casual twist, wedges are the way to go. They're especially ideal for women who want a lift but don't enjoy wearing heels. Pair them with wrap dresses, trousers, or loungy pants. A popular summer pick, wedges come in dressier styles like leather and suede or more sporty versions in canvas. These are also a flattering choice for Dainties and

Curvies since they lengthen the silhouette by drawing attention downward toward your feet.

SLIDES: With a nod to old Hollywood, these sexy little numbers really go with anything from frilly skirts and shift dresses to wide-leg pants and capri jeans. Stick with a slender heel and a banded instep with a flattering curve that covers your feet, with enough support so that you don't end up easily "sliding" out of them and onto the floor. Flirty embellishments like small buckles, beading, and knots add kick. Slides flatter lots of bodies, from Booties to Dainties, by giving a slim feminine shape to the leg.

PLATFORMS: When you want to make a statement, slide into a pair of these. The chunky heel and "platform" base offer a glamorous retro look that works with an empire-waist dress, wide-leg slacks, and boot-cut jeans. We especially love them in dark suedes and rich leathers—small accents like braiding or two-tone designs can funk things up a bit. With the ultra-high base, these aren't for the faint of heart, but the added height can do wonders to slenderize a thicker ankle and add definition to the lower bod.

SLINGBACKS: Ladylike and alluringly sexy, these are a perfect pick for gals who prefer a bit more security since the heel strap helps your foot stays put. Whichever size heel you choose, look for something refined that narrows at the tip. This is the ideal shoe to pair with breezy flutter-sleeve dresses, linen pants, and pencil skirts. Slingbacks come in open- and close-toe options and are a flirty look no matter what your shape.

No Kidding

If you have a small foot (size 6½ and below), you may strike gold in the kids' department, where there are lots of great-looking finds (especially sneakers and flats) and the prices are oh-so-alluring (less than for the adults). Youth sizes can be just the right fit, and you'll be surprised at the stylish options available. Who knows? You may even find yourself swapping shoes with your little ones!

PEEP-TOES: We can't resist the flirty name of this shoe. The look is all about letting the toes peep through, but how much they show is what makes them ultra-stylish. The higher the heel, the more impact. You want just enough "toe cleavage" to be alluring but not enough to make your piggies look crammed. Peep-toes have a slight vintage flair that's timeless and works just as well with dressy silk evening pants as it does with trouser-cut jeans and a tunic top. And slip these on with a long halter dress for an evening look that defines "dressed to kill"!

SANDALS: Strappy, sassy, and super-sexy, these are the best way to really show off your tootsies when you're in the mood. There are so many variations on the sandal—from tall and tantalizing to soft and sophisticated kitten heels. The thinner the straps the more modern they're going to look. Check out the cut around the toes: you want something that curves and flatters your foot. Sandals go with anything and everything, and have a magical ability to "loosen up" what could otherwise be a conservative outfit—red sandals can spice up pinstripe pants and a white button-down . . . snakeskin heels can transform plain-old jeans-and-a-tee . . . and metallic bronze flats can take your beach look from so-so to sizzling!

BALLET FLATS: If you haven't noticed by now, we love heels. But there are times when we're in the mood for a little more comfort. That's when we conjure up our inner Audrey Hepburn and reach for a pair of ballet flats. The girly silhouette and modern styling takes an otherwise plain shoe and makes it playful. Slip these on with capris, slim jeans, a flowing skirt, or a summery spaghetti-strap dress. For the most comfort, look for buttery soft, malleable leathers that conform to your foot. Embellishments and prints add pizzazz—medallions, bows, buttons, leopard, or embroidered touches. Gals of every size from sweet petite Dainties to divinely tall Leggies will love the comfy cool vibe of ballet flats.

FLIP-FLOPS: If we were stranded on a deserted island and allowed to take only one pair of shoes with us, this would be the type we'd pick. It's an easy choice. What would be hard would be deciding on which pair. The iconic rubber flip-flop has evolved into metallic flats, terry thongs, and pretty little numbers with beads and baubles. Even if you don't live in California (as we do), flip-flops are a staple. Wear them around the house, with yoga pants and a cozy V-neck. Sport them with jeans and tees . . . airy warm-weather dresses . . . tunics and slacks . . . and casual skirts with tanks. Dainties look-ing for a little lift or Booties and Hipsters looking to balance their lower bod can stock up on wedge styles that add height (in everything from rubber to faux suede). Whatever flavor you favor, flip-flops aren't just for the beach anymore!

BOOTS: The queen diva of the shoe world, boots are instant attitude. Leather, suede, high or low—they are a definite wardrobe essential. Every girl should own at least one pair of black leather high-heel boots that hit just below the knee. Wear them on the outside of fitted, straight leg jeans with a feminine blouse or underneath boot-leg pants and a jacket. They also work wonders with a wrap dress and can kick up a skirt-and-sweater combo. Look for rich supple leather, a thin to medium heel, and a sleek fit through the ankle and leg. Other styles we gravitate to are a stacked heel with bunched leather (pairs perfectly with jeans), and platforms that make a statement while adding extra height. Flat boots can be a sassy, comfy pick with jeans or skirts, and ankle boots look fresh with pants—just the right alternative when you want the low-maintenance vibe of a boot without the extra bells and whistles.

SNEAKERS: With an endless array of styles and colors, sneakers have truly moved into the spotlight. We're not talking about the bulky all-white cross-trainers either. The modern versions include racing numbers with zippy colors (like red, green, hot pink, and silver) and Velcro straps (in place of laces), ballet styles, and Mary Janes. There's definitely something for everyone. Wear them with loungy looks and jeans, or create a relaxed sophisticated look by pairing Con-verse with flat-front trousers and a button-down.

BAGS 101

SHOULDER BAG: The versatility and casually chic style of shoulder bags make them the workhorses of our everyday wardrobe. They go with just about everything from jeans and a crisp button-down to a shift or sundress. They're roomy enough to carry all your daily essentials as you're running to work or er-rands but slim enough to transition into a night out.

Slouchy hobos lend a slightly bohemian flair, zippered satchels add a cosmopolitan edge, and flap-over styles with magnetic or buckle closures give a feminine touch. Chain handles, small outside pockets, and other details offer endless variety. And while shoulder bags come in many different lengths, we suggest sticking with something that hits at or above the waist, or close under the arm. Wearing your bag close against your upper body creates a less bulky silhouette (plus, it's a safer way to carry it in busy shopping malls or on crowded city streets).

HANDBAG: Handbags are the ultimate ladylike accessories . . . they tend to be more delicate and refined than other types, and the simple act of carrying a purse in your hand just feels girly and sophisticated. Look for accents that enhance: chain or bamboo handles, framed styles, and old-fashioned ball clasps. Handbags are the ideal way to add a vintage touch to dresses or refined femininity to pencil skirts and cardigans. And for those looking to play up their lower bod, they can even add a bit of oomph to that area.

TOTE: For those gals who find themselves carrying more and more stuff all the time (from magazines and cosmetics to laptops, baby gear, and mobile phones), a good basic tote is a must. Soft, unframed styles can actually soften your silhouette, offering a sizable bag without the heft and hard lines of a framed style. Whether open or zipped, totes take us from work to weekend in a snap—and they can easily look casual or dressy, especially versions made of soft supple leathers or classic suedes. Basic blacks and browns are trusty neutrals to have in your stash, and a more colorful tote can add punch to your seasonal spring and summer wardrobes. Plus we love the fact that you can hand-carry a tote or toss it over your shoulder when you're really on the go!

CLUTCH: While they've typically been thought of as more of an evening bag, clutches are a fun choice for any time of day—especially if you don't need to lug a bunch of loot. Perfect for daytime dates, movie nights out with the girls, or casual brunches. And because they're so slim and small, you can play around with the design. Textured or patent leathers, beads and embellishments, metallics, and other elements make clutches anything but dull! They are a super-stylish choice when you want to carry a few essentials without adding the bulk or weight of a larger bag.

BAUBLES 101

NECKLACES: From long and layered to short and chunky—chokers, pendants, lariats, and everything in between—necklaces are one of the most feminine accessories you can throw on and one of the quickest ways to instantly turn a piece of clothing into an "outfit." Aside from giving your boobs a boost, necklaces can balance out your upper body by creating a vertical line, drawing attention upward or downward, or adding a minimizing delicate touch or a maximizing dramatic edge. Necklaces have amazing powers of transformation: they can take a plain T-shirt from casual to classy . . . a men's style vest from stiff to sassy . . . and a simple gauze dress from sweet to sexy. Among the essentials that every girl should have: long gold chains for layering, gold pendants for layering or wearing alone, a chunky gold or bead necklace that works on its own, a diamond or CZ solitaire, and a handful of "fun" pieces (vintage-inspired lockets, crosses, and such).

Belt One Out

There are so many ways to go with a belt—whether worn traditionally through belt loops, low-slung at the hips over a loose tunic, or wrapped sash-style with a dress. Belts can have a major shaping impact on your silhouette. They can help define the waistline, break up a long torso, soften a belly bulge, or flatter curvy feminine hips. A medium-width belt (around two inches) flatters most body shapes from Curvies to Dainties. Gals looking to accentuate their shapely figures might try a flirty blouse paired with a pencil skirt and a wide belt. And Leggies can rock it in a tunic dress or form-fitted sweater dress with a low-slung woven leather belt.

Wrap and Roll

Sure, they help keep you warm, but scarves and wraps are also a smart way to punch up a look. A colorful or printed scarf tied loosely around the neck (and hitting around the belly button) not only adds pizzazz but can also draw attention to your upper body or create a longer, leaner line. And a lightweight cashmere, brushed cotton, or silk-blend wrap can be a sophisticated option when it's cool out but you don't want the extra weight of a jacket. Plus it helps soften your shoulder, bust, and belly area.

EARRINGS: When it comes to earrings, simple styles can often be the most stunning. Diamond studs, pearls, gold hoops—it's hard to go wrong. In addition to these staples, play around with drop earrings (including some with delicate gemstones), ethnic-inspired scroll earrings, and mod variations on the hoops. Whatever style you choose, earrings help to brighten and accentuate your face and neck. It's a quick and easy way to customize your look: a simple black wrap dress can go a dozen ways depending on your jewelry picks. Just remember to choose earrings that enhance and don't overpower.

BRACELETS: There's something really sexy about wearing a few chunky bangles—and it instantly dresses up any outfit. Play with gold, silver, and enamel styles. Cuff bracelets are also a versatile staple. Rummage through your grandma's drawers for an oldie but goodie with vintage flair. A diamond tennis bracelet pairs perfectly with anything, from jeans to an evening gown. And we can't resist the playfulness of a charm bracelet with relaxed, casual looks like cargo pants and a tee, or a breezy summer dress.

WATCH: Sure they tell the time, but watches can also be quite the fashion statement. Wear a silver oversized men's style with pants and a button-down or even yoga pants and flip-flops. No worries if it's a little big—just let it dangle on your wrist like a bracelet. Strap on a dainty gold cuff watch for a dressed-up evening out. Or mix some fun color into your casual weekend wardrobe with a chunky watch in pink, blue, or red.

RINGS: Rings are a fun, accessible way to play up your style. You can go big and bold by wearing one oversized cocktail ring with anything from pants and jackets to jeans and button-downs, and of course any cocktail attire. Or create your own look by stacking a few dainty designs on your digits. Exotic vintage-inspired pieces can also become the centerpiece of any outfit. So go ahead, ring it on!

Keep Your Cool

Chilly weather doesn't have to mean hiding under layers of body-padding bulk. You can bundle up while still staying sleek and stylish. Skullcaps or knit hats that hug the head look sassy. Try allowing a few chunks or curls of hair to peek out and frame your face. Keep the look modern with leather and suede gloves that have a cozy lining. Finish it off with a classic neutral scarf in black, tan, or chocolate brown. (We love cashmere, and you can find it at all different price points.)

Conclusion

Regardless of the "standards" that seem to come with every age, beautiful comes in so many shapes and sizes. Whether you have a robust rump, teeny tiny boobies, Hail Mary hips, or any other glorious figure "flaunt," we hope you'll feel inspired to shop and to look at your clothes in new, adventurous ways.

You may have noticed that we never used the word "hide" or "camouflage" in this book. Or that annoying word *don't*. (There's nothing more discouraging than being told you shouldn't wear something because of your shape.)

Once you learn to love your body, you're halfway to revealing your most sexy self. From there, build your perfect closet by stocking up on trusty basics that make you feel and look your most sublime. The Hall of Famers we spoke about are the essentials that we can't get enough of—boot-leg jeans, sumptuous V-necks, curve-lovin' wrap dresses, and heels that make any woman feel like a goddess.

Then pepper in trendy items to add flair or a little something unexpected—the current hot handbag, a seasonal scarf, that funky belt, or some sassy bangles. Those little extras can add big impact just where you want it, whether it's your neck, cleavage, hips, or tootsies. A pair of yellow heels, a long gold necklace, and a colorful suede handbag can easily punch up any look.

Experiment and play. Mix things up. And always remember that alluring style doesn't have to cost a lot. The basics we share throughout this book are available for all budgets.

Now prepare to take the fear out of fashion and put the fabulous in!

———

SOURCES

Stores and Websites

Target (www.target.com)
Anthropologie
   (www.anthropologie.com)
Club Monaco (www.clubmonaco.com)
Urban Outfitters
   (www.urbanoutfitters.com)
J.Crew (www.jcrew.com)
Banana Republic
   (www.bananarepublic.com)
Nordstrom (www.nordstrom.com)
Zara (www.zara.com)
Express (www.express.com)
BCBG Max Azria (www.bcbg.com)
m.frederic (www.mfredric.com)
Victoria's Secret
   (www.victoriassecret.com)
Lucky Brand
   (www.luckybrandjeans.com)
Gap/Gap Body (www.gap.com)
Old Navy (www.oldnavy.com)
Everything But Water
   (www.everythingbutwater.com)
Vix Swimwear
   (www.vixswimwear.com)
Lululemon (www.lululemon.com)
Athleta (www.athleta.com)
Shopbop (www.shopbop.com)
Revolve Clothing
   (www.revolveclothing.com)

Pink Mascara
   (www.pinkmascara.com)
Rapunzel's (www.shoprapunzels.com)
Boden USA (www.bodenusa.com)
Basic Boutique
   (www.basicboutique.com)
Hollister (www.hollisterco.com)
Maya Brenner Jewelry
   (www.mayabrenner.com)
Inhabit chunky knits
   (www.inhabitny.com)
Zappos (www.zappos.com)
Piperlime (piperlime.com)
Havaianas (www.havaianasus.com)

Jeans

AG Jeans
Joe's Jeans
James Jeans
Paige Premium Denim
Citizens of Humanity
Rock & Republic

Tees

Velvet (luxurious tees)
James Perse (soft and sumptuous
   tees)

Clothing

Calypso (amazing knits)

Alexander Wang (cozy cashmere)

Jenni Kayne (sexy tunics)

Philip Lim (gorgeous modern dresses)

Diane von Furstenberg (amazing wrap dresses)

Michael by Michael Kors (sophisticated classics)

Nanette Lepore (feminine pieces with flair)

Trina Turk (hip, flattering designs)

Mint (modern clothing with a slight edge)

Porridge (girly tops and dresses)

Antik Batik (sensual clothing with an ethnic touch)

Lingerie

Medela

Le Mystere

Chantelle

Warners

Vanity Fair

Olga

Wacoal

Fantasie

Fayreform

Natori

Hanky Panky

Spanx

Shoes

Puma

Belle by Sigerson Morrison

Circa Joan & David

Converse

Delman

Jessica Simpson

Steve Madden

INDEX